A single NVA soldier appeared in the grass only twenty feet above us and fired a long burst that raked across the back of Clark's legs. He howled in pain, but our situation was so desperate that we could not stop shooting to help him; one less bullet from our rifles and the NVA would walk on our corpses. With bullets flying everywhere and sinister shapes snaking through the long grass, an NVA soldier, so low to the ground he was almost crawling, came shooting his way toward us. From off to one side Finn fired at the enemy soldier, who was almost at the end of his rifle barrel. The bullets ripped out his throat and sent him bouncing and thrashing about on the ground before a quick if not painless death.

Mac and I knew that the spot we were in was no place to be. . . .

Books published by The Ballantine Publishing Group
are available at quantity discounts on bulk purchases
for premium, educational, fund-raising, and special
sales use. For details, please call 1-800-733-3000.

THE WAR
IN I CORPS

Richard A. Guidry

IVY BOOKS • NEW YORK

An Ivy Book
Published by The Ballantine Publishing Group
Copyright © 1998 by Richard A. Guidry

http://www.randomhouse.com

Library of Congress Catalog Card Number: 97-93917

ISBN 0-8041-1692-X

Manufactured in the United States of America

First Edition: February 1998

10 9 8 7 6 5 4 3 2 1

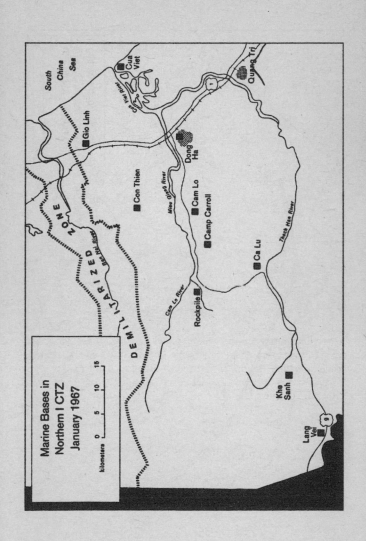

Marine Bases in
Northern I CTZ
January 1967

kilometers 0   5   10   15

DEMILITARIZED ZONE

South China Sea

Cua Viet

Cua Viet River

Gio Linh

Quang Tri

Con Thien

Dong Ha

Ben Hai River

Mieu Giang River

Cam Lo

Camp Carroll

Cam Lo River

Rockpile

Ca Lu

Thach Han River

Khe Sanh

Lang Vei

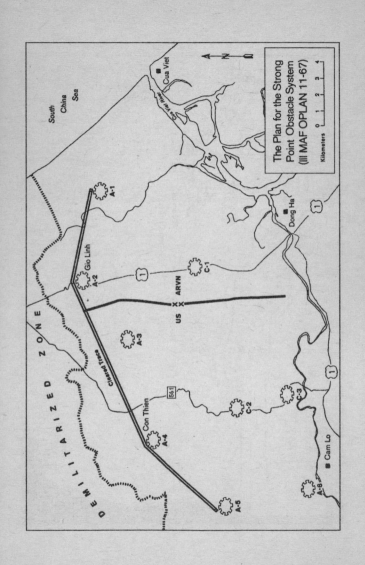

The Plan for the Strong Point Obstacle System (III MAF OPLAN 11-67)

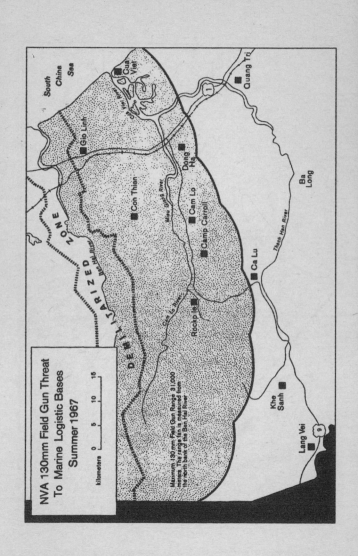

NVA 130mm Field Gun Threat
To Marine Logistic Bases
Summer 1967

kilometers 0   5   10   15

South China Sea

Cua Viet

Gio Linh

DEMILITARIZED ZONE

Con Thien

Dong Ha

Cam Lo

Camp Carroll

Ca Lu

Rockpile

Khe Sanh

Lang Vei

Quang Tri

Ba Long

Thach Han River

Maximum 130mm Field Gun Range 31,000 meters. The arc of fire is projected from the north bank of the Ben Hai River

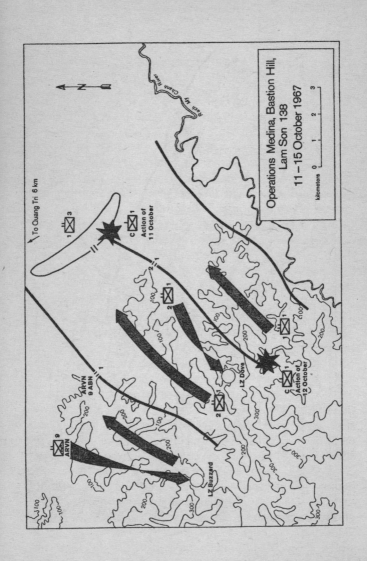

Operations Medina, Bastion Hill, Lam Son 138
11–15 October 1967

kilometers
0   1   2   3

Prologue

For some reason, the morning coffee did not go down well. It had smelled good, but left a queasy discomfort in the pit of my stomach. Just the same, I left home determined to keep my job on its monotonous stride.

The museum was even more boring than usual. It was nearly deserted except for a few dedicated art lovers and indomitable tourists who would not be dissuaded by the rumble of thunder that rolled in from the nearby Pacific. I passed the gloomy morning with little to do but listen to the tap of heels on the hard marble floor and the chime of the antique clock on the floor above.

Though long in coming, lunchtime was merciful relief from the crushing boredom of the morning. I turned my collar up against a light rain as I headed for the little café just outside the main gallery and, once there, found a dark corner to quietly enjoy a cup of orange-flavored tea. I had to forgo a more substantial lunch, because my stomach was in such a state of gastric flutter that I could endure only the lightest refreshment. Through a window streaked with rain and dust, I searched the green pine-covered hills of the Pacific Palisades for nothing in particular, maybe for some relief from the nauseated tingle that radiated around the edge of my body, but saw only ghosts in the mist.

On the way back to the gallery, I was stopped by a well-dressed old woman who asked, "Is the Etruscan Zeus mounted on marble or alabaster?"

"It's mounted on polished granite," I answered. My words stopped me cold. "Today is Granite Day," I said aloud.

Chapter 1

Late in the evening of October 26, 1967, Battalion 1/4 assembled near the gates of a small, muddy, fungi-covered support base called Camp Evans, ready to embark on an excursion code-named "Operation Granite." Operations were anything but the precise surgical actions implied by the name. Instead, they were noisy, blundering, blunt instruments, too slow and too clumsy to catch an enemy who did not want to be caught. Just the same, I welcomed a chance to get out of the musty little bog situated just southeast of the city of Hue. In a driving rain, laden with heavy packs, our platoon lumbered toward its place in the long line of men sprawled in the thick sticky mud. The drenching rains deterred few Marines from catching a few minutes' sleep before departure. When the whole circus was finally under one tent, we started a snake dance across the soggy plain toward mountains hidden by dark, low-hanging clouds.

Normally, I hated the rain, but on that occasion I welcomed it, hoping that the shower would wash away some of the Camp Evans grime. However, the rain only added a slimy quality to the crust of dirt and fungus that encased my body. Running my fingers across my arm was like following the tracks of a snail.

Even before Operation Granite started, I hated it. As usual, we were not told where we were headed, how long the trip would take, nor, most important, what kind of enemy we would face. I could only speculate according

3

to the nature of equipment that we carried. All that we were told was that we would explore the eastern approaches to Ashau Valley. In grunts' language that translated into nobody knew what would be out there so we were going to stumble around to see how much attention we would attract. I was an old salt by the time we walked out of Camp Evans, but more than half the men in the platoon were fresh in country and jittery about going on their first op. Noisy chatter up and down the line ceased as the long column of Marines lurched forward out onto the flat, bush-covered plain that preceded the mountains. We had marched a circuitous route through predawn darkness for about an hour when the stagnant air was punctuated by a shrill metallic ring. I hit the deck instantly, just ahead of a small explosion that went off near the front of the platoon. I listened for a second sound, that of gunfire, but heard nothing. I listened for some cry in the night, but still heard nothing. A few yards behind me, my friend Dennis McLean lifted his head from the mud and looked inquisitively toward me for an answer that I did not have. A few seconds later, Steve Lane, a squad leader, came back along the column with word that we were to return to the base.

The last vestige of drizzle mercifully ended on our return trip, but our spirits sank low when we learned what had brought us back. The limp bodies of Albert and Thompson were rushed to the infirmary, the victims of a bouncing Betty, a nasty little antipersonnel mine. Shards of sharp metal had perforated Albert's back and crushed Thompson's chest. Thompson, in the field only a few days, was already dead, and Albert survived only a few minutes more. Cloaked in the greenish glow of kerosene lamps, the whole company gathered in a large supply tent to say a collective prayer for the souls of our dead friends. A solemn chaplain said a well-worn benediction, then sent us on our way. We left the tent much sadder, but much more alert. All day we marched back and forth across the soggy plain, searching the thick brush for sign of enemy presence. Darkness once again closed in on us as we finally reached the foothills of the looming mountain. The battalion broke up into its four constituent companies and set up defensive circles about a mile apart. Alpha Company climbed the hills above us to take command of the high ground overlooking our positions.

Before the usual ritual of setting up watch rotations and digging in, I headed for the actual (platoon commander) to see if Lieutenant Johnson wanted to use the extra radio that I carried. I walked toward the center of the circle thinking that this operation carried the same mood as the countless others on which I had been—the short-timers (men near the end of their tours of duty) were tense because they knew what could happen, and the new guys were tense because they did not know.

McLean knew what could happen. He had just returned from a long convalescence thanks to an enemy grenade that sent hot shrapnel slicing into his side. After being wounded, he was assigned to a rear-echelon job, but unfounded pangs of guilt moved him to volunteer to accompany his old unit on the excursion into the mountains. He followed me toward the CP (command post), complaining of the bad weather and the paucity of information about the mission. Just another trip to nowhere, I assured him, full of sweat and leeches and not much more. Our long friendship betrayed my words, revealing an uncertain tone in my voice.

Just before we reached the CP, the rapid clatter of gunfire erupted from the hill just above us. My friend and I raced over to Abbot, the platoon radio operator, just in time to hear the frantic voice of Chambers, an old friend in Alpha Company. "We got caught in a bad spot! Got to pull back! Fire comin' at us from three sides!" Before the battalion CP could give the okay to pull back, the shooting stopped. Soon after the last tracer round sliced across the black sky, a sit-rep (situation report) came nervously over the radio. Much to our relief, there was no report of casualties. Just the usual night skirmish, two small units running into each other by accident, I thought. Just the same, the quiet that followed swept down from the hills like a cold north wind.

Back in the line, we noisily prepared for the arrival of the unseen enemy, scraping shallow holes in the hard gravel. Waiting sleeplessly through the night, the tense night passed to a gray, overcast dawn with no further contact with the enemy. In that part of the country, the enemy was most likely to be Viet Cong (VC) main forces, a category of enemy soldiers for whom we had little respect, rather than the NVA (North Vietnamese Army), whom we customarily fought. Fighting the NVA was like fighting a conventional war, a lot of maneuvering and firepower involved, but the VC were the ghosts in the mist.

In the dark gloom of early morning we started the arduous climb into the mountains, each company climbing a different hill. I was on point for our company. I was still wary from the shooting of the previous night, so all my senses were at their keenest when I came over the summit of the first slippery slope. My eyes strained at every tree and bush in search of some sign that the thick foliage ahead was concealment for a camouflaged enemy waiting in ambush. My ears strained to hear the faintest snap or rustle in the thick mat of dead foliage. There was only silence, except for the squawks of jungle birds high above in the canopy of tall trees.

Nearly every tree was scarred, chopped, and hacked by years of bombing, yet there were few craters on the forest floor. Between the trees was a thick entanglement of vines and bushes, almost impenetrable except for a few open spaces. Following riverlets of gurgling water through one of the openings, I came upon a wide clearing between two steeply rising mountains. Fresh footprints on one side of the temporary stream leaped out at my eyes. In a rush of alarm, I fell to the ground and jammed my M-16 to my shoulder.

Behind me, the rest of the squad disappeared into the short brush in similar fashion. Lane scrambled forward in a high crawl. I pointed to the fresh footprints in the soft mud, then to the depression in the brush to which it led. He silently motioned the first fire team (a three-man subdivision of a squad) to the left, then bolted across the clearing toward the depression in the bush. I followed instinctively. The rest of the squad automatically came forward and got in line with rifles pointed toward the clearing. We crashed headlong into the brush, ready to fire away at anything before us, but, fortunately, nothing was there. Our pell-mell dash was not simply foolhardy bravado, but a quickly calculated risk in pursuit of an elusive enemy. The footprints told us enough to justify the risk. The number of prints, the sharp edges, the direction they pointed, and the spaces between each print told of three or four people who had run away just minutes ahead of our arrival.

At times like those, our senses were so keen that they seemed magical. You get Superman eyes, you can perceive things like a shark. Your whole body becomes one big antenna. A small green bag left in the bushes was cautiously examined. It was filled with rice, a confirmation of the hasty departure of a small group of enemy troops. Our new platoon commander, Lieutenant Johnson, reported our discovery as the probable presence of an enemy reconnaissance team, then deployed our platoon into a slow-moving wedge formation for the ascent up the next slope.

The formation afforded greater protection to our flanks, but was almost impossible to maintain in the rugged terrain. Movement slowed to a crawl. Struggling through a thicket of brush and vines, Private Johnson slipped off a slick rock and fell backward into a shallow depression. Lucky not to be a few pounds heavier, he rested on top of a mat of foliage which concealed a deep crevasse that ran to the top of the mountain. In rescuing Private Johnson, someone spotted an earthen bunker near the top of the mountain, and the tension of the previous night returned.

We crept slowly upward, keeping low to the ground and seeking the cover of rocks and trees, like predators stalking a wary herd. The bunkers were found to be empty; we breathed more easily.

At the bottom of the mountain, we paused for our only meal of the day before climbing the next. I saved most of my rations for later in the day and ate only tiger shit (an oily swirl of grape jelly and peanut butter spread over a ball of pasty white bread). I took the occasion to clean my M-16 and to talk with McLean about the futility of using flatland formations in the mountains. He and I had been together since just after boot camp, and I'd never heard him gripe with such vigor. I took his complaining to be nervousness about his return to the field after such a long absence. Also, he had been close with Albert, and I suspected that Albert's death still lingered with him. That was a great danger, because the bush had a way of ensnaring anyone with fleeting concentration. To lighten his mood, I explained that Detroit, his hometown, was more dangerous than any part of Vietnam. Unappreciative of my humor, he brushed his thick red hair back with his muddy hands until it was plastered to his head, and continued griping.

"Will you let the lieutenant run the platoon?" Corporal Lane said in his distinct Long Island accent as he shooed McLean back to his own squad.

We started up the next mountain with our platoon again spread widely in an awkward wedge formation to protect the rest of the company, which followed in a long column. We soon found a natural trail that had been carved by rainwater and landslides. It was littered with fallen trees and boulders, but, like the crevasse on the previous mountain, it offered an easy climb to the top of the mountain. Taking advantage of the discovery, Lieutenant Johnson shifted us to a column formation. As soon as we stepped on the trail, shots rang out, sending everyone diving for cover. From the head of the column the rapid clatter of several M-16s answered the pop of an AK-47. After a few minutes of silence our platoon came onto the trail and followed the second platoon up the mountain, tensed for more shooting.

A few yards up the trail I saw why the shooting stopped so abruptly. A solitary VC with a string of bullet holes across his chest lay propped against a tree to one side of the trail. He looked young, a teenager like most of us, I supposed. All he wore were red shorts and rubber sandals. I was surprised that his red shorts did not show well against the dark jungle. For certain, the fellow was not all alone in the middle of the jungle mountains, so further contact was expected. Lieutenant Karzchewski, commander of the second platoon, thought the dead man was a part of the recon team we had earlier put to flight, but I thought not. It seemed that the VC had deliberately put himself in harm's way.

When we neared the top of the mountain, an earthen bunker, partially uncovered by recent rains, was spotted by the point man. "Machine gun up," came the call from the front of the column. Word was passed down line that Burnhart, the gunner, was to recon by fire. Since there had been shooting only moments earlier, there was little reason to keep quiet. Still, there was a long wait while the company commander sought permission to fire. Lieutenant Johnson sent Cardoluzzi and me forward so that Lieutenant Karzchewski could have extra rockets and a radio at his disposal. Just as we arrived at the head of the column, Burnhart stepped onto the middle of the trail, out in the open, as if he knew the bunkers were empty. With his M-60 at his side, he waited for permission to recon by fire.

Like a sudden clap of thunder, a terrible torrent of enemy fire poured down from the bunkers. It looked as if hundreds of bullets smashed into Burnhart at once, sending him flying backward as though hit by a freight train. Bullets slammed into Lieutenant Karzchewski, ripping off the top of his shoulder, spinning him around and knocking him off his feet. He tried to stand, but a string of machine gun bullets burst into his back and exploded his chest into a mass of red.

"Stay close!" I shouted to Cardoluzzi, but I doubted that he heard me above the tremendous roar of gunfire. From behind the cover of a large tree, I tried to radio our platoon, but the radio did not work. I fired a few quick unaimed shots in the direction of the bunkers, then ducked back behind the tree. From the other side of the tree, Cardoluzzi fired a LAW (light antitank weapon). The small rocket exploded against the bunker in a geyser of smoke and dust, but the whistling bullets kept coming. Three men, rifles blazing like blowtorches, dashed from the bunker, and I fired four quick shots at them before my rifle jammed. Fortunately for me, the three VC were cut down.

From another position, far across on an adjacent mountain, bullets peppered the tree behind which Cardoluzzi had taken cover. I bounded from behind the tree, waving my diminutive friend along. I took only one step when a blinding white flash erupted from the tree, sending me tumbling out into a small clearing below the trail. I lay on the ground, my face pressed against the soft wet grass, the roar of battle reduced to a shrill ring. Hastened by the dull thump of bullets into the ground at my fingertips, I desperately fought back a drift into unconsciousness. Only the concealment provided by the short waving grass shielded me from the blizzard of missiles.

I pushed life back into my legs and scrambled back up to the trail, only to find Cardoluzzi still lying next to the tree. Facedown with his hands clasped tightly against his ears, he appeared to be frozen with fear. "Get out of here!" I yelled at him. But an awful sight cut short my breath. The whole lower part of his face was gone and blood gurgled from a fist-size hole in his throat. I looked down the trail for help and was further shocked by the sight of dead and wounded Marines spilled all over the mountain. Bullets thrashed the nearby brush with such intensity that I knew someone was shooting at me in particular. All around me bullets sang a loud ricocheting howl as they skimmed off trees and rocks. If I stayed where I was, a bullet would soon find me, but it would take a miracle to move through the intense fire.

Just as I decided on a suicidal dash, men from my platoon came charging straight up the middle of the trail, firing furiously at the bunkers at the top of the hill and all but ignoring the position to the left. They did not come as high on the trail as I was, but their intense gunfire suppressed the bunkers enough for me to race to a big rock farther down the trail. From there I leapfrogged from rock to rock until I reached the others. Some men pulled the wounded to safety while others kept up the furious counterfire. Just as I reached the platoon, Lane was directing his squad toward the downhill side of the trail to come up on the bunkers from the flank; however, I stopped them with a warning that they were walking right into fire from an enemy position on the adjacent mountain.

From behind whatever cover we could find, we fought furiously to overcome the extreme disadvantage in which we found ourselves. To the right of the trail, the mountain rose steeply with thick jungle; to the left it sloped sharply downward and was dotted with small open patches. The unseen enemy fired from well-entrenched positions at the top of the mountain and from the mountains to the left. I exchanged rifles with Private Jones, who had been with the platoon only two weeks. Jones had taken a large, painful wound in one thigh, but hardly grimaced.

Among the thick jungle to the right, Frost spotted the feet of well-camouflaged enemy soldiers as they struggled downhill. All those near the front of the column shifted their fire to the right, where the VC were so close that one of them tumbled onto the trail no more than a yard in front of the rock behind which I'd taken cover, his blood flowing past my nostrils. With that diversion, fire came from the bunkers with renewed vigor. Corporal Johnson, leader of the second squad, started another push at the bunkers while we worked over the group to the right. Slowly, he moved upward, dragging the rest of the platoon behind him until they were near the place where Cardoluzzi lay dead. Skinny Doc White grabbed our dead friend by the collar and dragged him a few feet downhill, but had to let go and dive for cover to avoid a long string of machine-gun fire.

"Pull back!" Lieutenant Johnson shouted, trying desperately to be heard above the deafening gunfire, but bullets crashed into the young lieutenant's chest and jerked him from underneath a waving hand, making the order his last. At nearly the same moment, Corporal Johnson caught three bullets in the stomach. Remarkably, he kept his feet and stumbled to cover behind the rock he had just left. Just after Corporal Johnson was hit, Private Dickens made a long panicky dash down the middle of the trail, but he stayed in the open too long; a single bullet smashed into the back of his neck and came out of his mouth in a spray of blood and tissue. He fell over a fallen tree, spilling his life into the dark earth.

Two new guys, Clark and Hunter, crowded close to me and mimicked my every move. "Take'm down, Gitch!" Lane shouted to start the withdrawal of his squad. Doc White had already started to weave his way downhill with Corporal Johnson draped over his bony back. Brabender was not so lucky. He'd been struck in the side as he leaped from one rock to another. Someone pressed a bandage against the blood-spurting wound, but he was soon a lemon-yellow corpse.

To help cover our withdrawal, the gunnery sergeant picked up an M-60 from a dead machine gunner, but before he could get off a shot, a bullet sliced off his thumb and splashed his own blood back into his face. Sergeant Burcher, our platoon sergeant, reached for the M-60, but a bullet slid across the back of his neck, slicing it open like a sharp knife across an overripe tomato. He was very lucky; a centimeter more and he would have been killed. Luck turned the other way for Private Johnson. Though he was well covered behind two large boulders, a ricocheting bullet struck him in the temple, killing him instantly.

We were shot up very badly, but the platoon held its integrity as we inched down the mountain. With Sergeant Burcher wounded and Lieutenant Johnson dead, Lane took control of the platoon. A little farther down the mountain the shooting blended to one reverberating roar. From across the mountain to the left, the flaming tails of rockets arced over the short distance and exploded in thunderous clouds of smoke. We used the smoke to quicken our withdrawal. I snatched Doc White away from the corpse of Petersen as he vainly tried to breathe life into him, then scurried a few yards lower before the smoke cleared. Hunter held up well, but the vacant look on Clark's face told me that he was next in line for a bullet if he was left to himself. I told him that he had performed well up to that point and that he would survive if he just kept doing the same thing. He took my assurance as the Word of God, and his attentiveness seemed to return. However, I did not believe my own words. I was sure that hordes of enemy troops would come pouring out of the bunkers and kill all of us.

With our ammunition dwindling dangerously and casualties mounting, my expectation seemed about to be fulfilled when enemy troops came out of the bunkers to maintain close contact with us as we withdrew. The contact was too close for three VC, who were dropped in the middle of the trail. For some reason, everyone started yelling at the top of their lungs, some screaming obscenities while others just yelled in anger. One squad fired suppressing cover while another inched backward, all the while everyone yelling. A flurry of RPGs (rocket propelled grenades) struck the middle of the trail and showered us with rocks and debris, slowing further withdrawal.

Lieutenant Goldman, a forward air controller, came up to our platoon to try to place illumination rounds above the mountain and to get HE (high explosives) on the summit. But it was a mission that he would never call; he and his radio operator were shot to death soon after they arrived. However, Abbot was able to finish the message that the lieutenant had started. Soon illumination rounds popped high overhead. With the coming of darkness, our need to see where we were going and where the enemy was overshadowed the need for concealment.

Shafts of yellow light punched through the canopy of tall trees as we slipped cautiously downward. It was a sad caravan that stumbled along the rocky trail. Wounded men occasionally cried out when the pain of their mutilated bodies was too much to bear in silence. The conditions of many of the wounded were so desperate that we stopped halfway down the trail to try to cut an LZ (landing zone) to get them out by helicopter, but after only a few minutes of furious hacking, it became clear that the effort yielded too little results.

Shots grew more infrequent as we moved lower on the mountain. As we again started downhill, the first HE rounds impacted on top of the mountain, sending large chunks of metal slashing through the trees. To make it through a firefight only to be killed by our own artillery was my greatest fear, the kind of irony so common to Vietnam.

We carried so many wounded that most of the dead were left behind. That ate at my guts. I felt very ashamed that my dear friend, Cardoluzzi, was left behind, his handsome face hacked into a grotesque mess of ragged flesh. I stumbled down the mountain, wondering how his mother would feel, the mother who had sounded so much like my own.

After what seemed an interminable trek, we reached a place at the base of the mountain where the wounded could be evacuated. So many in our platoon were lifted away by the old HU-34s that those of us who remained were divided between the other two platoons. When the growling clatter of the helicopters was reduced to a dull thump in the distance, an enormous explosion sent shock waves quaking through the mountains. From very high in the dark night sky, radar-directed, unseen, and unheard jets brought down a calamitous curtain on our day of infamy.

As Sergeant Shaw, sergeant for the second platoon, escorted the bedraggled remains of our platoon to different places in the defensive circle, I searched the vacant faces for my friend McLean. Hunter quietly took the place to which he was assigned, but Clark adamantly refused to be separated from what he thought had brought him through the day. The sergeant had hoped to use me in place of his dead radio operator, but the radio I carried had a big hole in it.

Soon after we were in place, Doc White came around to look after the lesser wounded to see who would be evacuated the next day.

"Where is everybody?" I asked anxiously.

"It was mostly the new guys who got killed," he answered with a cold bluntness uncommon to him, but told me what I'd been unwilling to ask.

"Have you seen Little Mac?"

"I don't know," he answered as he mechanically treated the cuts on my hands and face. He disappeared without easing my fear that the ugly black mountain had swallowed my dear friend.

When I could stand the doubt no longer, I left Clark to dig a hole and went to find someone who could tell me if McLean was dead or just wounded. As I groped through the darkness just behind the lines, a familiar shape came close. "You dumbass, volunteering for a mission like this!" I said to my friend as we hugged each other with relief. After comparing a macabre list of dead and wounded, we hurried back to our places in the line. Not until then did I realize how much time had passed. The shooting had started around noon, and it was deep into the night when it was over, but the whole ugly episode seemed to have lasted no more than five minutes. Time had been suspended.

Chapter 2

We arrived in Vietnam in the late morning of April 6, 1967, aboard a chartered Continental Airlines 707, the end of a very boisterous journey. Everyone was in such a lighthearted mood that you would have thought we were headed for Disneyland rather than Vietnam. On every trip down the aisle, the poor stewardess had to slap away out-reaching hands. Except for a few Army soldiers huddled near the front of the plane, all the passengers were Marines who had trained together during advanced infantry training. So it had been one raucous party all the way across the Pacific. Though we had blown off plenty of steam in Okinawa with every kind of debauchery imaginable, the cabin of the big white plane still reso-nated with the sound of rattling dice and rippling cards when finally we touched down in Da Nang. Good Bookin' Barns was probably one of the few people to arrive in Vietnam already high.

Our first view of Vietnam was of flimsy plywood shacks shimmering in tropical heat across a sun-bleached runway, a sight not too different from Camp Pendleton. Once we were off the plane, a blast of hot, moist air brought the party to an end. A heavily starched corporal led the unorganized mob over to a row of shabby little plywood barracks on the edge of the runway, housing for troops in transit. We assembled into a haphazard forma-tion while a neatly dressed sergeant droned endlessly about instructions and regulations. No one paid much attention except for the parts about where we were to eat and sleep. We already had orders as to our destination, so all we had to find out was where and when to catch a plane. Full of pride, the fashion-plate sergeant told us what to do in case of incoming enemy fire, but we were more interested in getting out of the blazing sun. When dismissed, we got our gear from a nearby hangar and straggled to the barracks.

Only a few guys were headed for the same unit; most were scattered all over I Corps. That was the first faulty policy I saw implemented in Vietnam. Our political motives to fight were vague at best, but the bonds of long-sustained friendships could inspire ordinary people to extraordinary efforts.

McLean, Ciantar, and I were fortunate enough to have been assigned to the same unit. McLean was a little red-headed kid from Detroit, short and muscular, with a face full of Howdy Doody freckles. His disarming looks and outgoing personality made him a friend to almost everyone. Even people who were at odds about every-thing else found agreement in the delightfulness of his personality. A group of black guys from Chicago street gangs were at constant odds with a group of tough New York Italians, but both groups liked "Little Mac." Slightly taller than McLean, Ciantar was a dark-haired fellow from Chicago who enjoyed saying that he was the toughest Maltese in the unit.

Soon our little plywood hut became a meeting place where old friends told well-worn jokes, said melancholy farewells, and recounted some of the misadventures that we'd shared. A favorite story told and retold was that of my seventy-five-dollar date. While on liberty at a beach near San Diego, I met a nice young lady who was a student at Chapman College. On our last liberty call before shipping out, many of the guys in our unit went down to Tijuana to pick up prostitutes while the rest went up to Los Angeles to work the disco circuit. On my last date, I went to a formal dance at Chapman College with Carmen. Peculiar for the barracks, my formal attire attracted a lot of attention and promoted a lot of questions.

"The boy is goin' to do some heavy waxin' tonight," Good Bookin' Barns said in barracks language that referred to an intense sexual episode. "I would go into that ho tonight and wouldn't come out till Sunday," he said with a big gold-toothed grin.

When Carmen called from the front of the barracks, where we usually met, I had her drive around to the side, explaining that I did not want to get my tuxedo dirty. In reality, I just wanted my roommates to get a good look at her. In a gleaming little green MG and a low-cut dress, she pulled every head in the barracks to the window.

As I left for the dance, Good Bookin' Barns brushed the shoulders of my coat and quietly reminded, "Lay it to her, bro."

When we were once again back in the barracks, stories of wild times abounded, those of sexual exploits and fights given special emphasis. After Contrell, a big country boy from Texas, told a very funny story about how he got beaten up by a monkey at a traveling carnival, he reminded the half-intoxicated assembly of Carmen's beauty.

"Where did you cop that hamma?" Yak inquired, the others crowding around my bunk to hear the answer. "She wus all-time monster cold-blooded, I know yo' chess is light as a feather?" he asked in anticipation of a savory story, suggesting I'd been sexually relieved.

Over the clamor of questions about Chapman College and the women there, Barns, true to his background as an emerging Dallas pimp, asked how much the date had cost me. When I answered seventy-five dollars, the onlookers were stunned. At that time, seventy-five dollars was more than two weeks' pay for a PFC. Barns chuckled, put his hand on my shoulder, and said, "Chumps lak this is gon' make me rich."

"Put a cover on that, I want to hear how he screwed that ho till she went blind," Yak said to Barns.

"As a matter of fact, we didn't make love at all," I replied. They fell over on the bunks, howling with laughter.

"I pulled a bitch like that out of the Whiskey A Go-Go. It's gon' take her a couple of days jest to walk straight," Barns hooted. "Seventy-five dollars and no pussy," he shouted.

"That's the trouble with you," I retorted. "You go out with bitches. Carmen is a refined young lady."

Wiping tears from his eyes, Yak said, "Keep the refined shit, give me the pussy." He shook his head in dismay. "Gitch, you sho is crazy," he said as they drifted back to their bunks.

That story and many others were told between the ear-cracking screams of jets that incessantly flew above the Da Nang airstrip. At the end of one of those stories, Grady came into the shack, two bulky suitcases under his long muscular arms. He dropped the bags in one corner and sat as inconspicuously as his tall frame would allow. When people started to filter away to the chow line, he lay on a cot and displayed a grin that I had come to know as a sign of trouble. After a while my fellow Texan started to pull items of clothing from the suitcases, glee-fully displaying them as if he had just been shopping at Saks, when actually he'd stolen the suitcases from offi-cers' quarters. The ivory-white jacket of a Navy com-mander showed that serious trouble could follow this prank. Angrily, I told him to get the things out of our hut and said that I was glad we were headed in different directions. He was very hurt and a bit puzzled. We'd been together for a very long time and were through mishaps a lot more serious than a few stolen clothes. I apologized and helped him stuff the clothes in a large plastic bag, then left for the mess hall. McLean and

Ciantar followed, not wanting to be found in the barracks with the pilfered garments.

From the chow line I noticed that the fellows washing the pots outside the mess were Vietnamese. I turned to McLean and said, "Isn't that just like Americans, always have to have someone cleaning up after them. Besides, those guys have a clear view of the runway."

"Just a minute before you start branding anyone an ugly American," Ciantar countered. "Who do you think is going to wash the damn pots, a bunch of pot washers from Kansas? Besides, these guys probably make more money than they ever dreamed of."

Unsatisfied with his retort, I eyed the Vietnamese suspiciously as we walked past. Ciantar lifted a small saucepan to his mouth as if to talk into a microphone. "Blue Leader, this is Blackbird," he said to make fun of my suspicion. The pot washers looked up from their work for only a second or two, presumably accustomed to the antics of American teenagers.

"If he's already paranoid, think what he's gonna be like when he leaves here," McLean said to Ciantar. Throughout the grand meal of gristle and grease, Ciantar complained about the poor quality of service cooking, recounting portions of his two years of study to become a chef.

On the way out of the mess hall we came upon a map that showed the locations of all the major fire support bases in I Corps, the northernmost of the four tactical zones into which South Vietnam was divided, and perhaps twenty percent of the country. I watched McLean's finger glide up the map until it finally hit the place for which we were destined. "My God! It's right on the border with North Vietnam," Ciantar said about Gio Linh.

"We'll be closer to Hanoi than Saigon," I said to my friend. To help digest that revelation as well as our meal, we headed off to the tent that was the EM (enlisted men's) club. At the door of the tent lay the very soiled jacket of a Navy commander. As we approached, two Marines jumped onto the jacket with both feet before entering the smoky little beer hall. The noise, the smoke, and the odor of stale beer did little for me, so I turned around and headed back for the barracks.

Alone in the barracks, I reflected on the circumstances that had brought me to Vietnam. Since my father's illness and subsequent death, I had been fully self-supporting, putting myself through the final year of high school by working as a night janitor at a local hospital. Not a week after graduation, I received notice from the Selective Service that I had been classified 1-A, that is, draft bait. Instead of the harbinger of doom that it was to so many, the notice offered some solution to the particularly difficult dilemma in which I found myself. I wanted to go to college, yet I needed to support myself. The two were mutually exclusive. I had gone to my high school counselor and made an impassioned plea to get help at securing the financial assistance I needed to go to college, but she hardly looked up from the papers through which she shuffled. "Do you know your feet stink?" was Mrs. Mock's only reply. When I tried to continue, she cut me off with a referral to a job to build mobile homes. At the time I had a scholarship offer from Texas Lutheran College, but only tuition was covered. A tour of duty in the service offered a solution to my troubles, but I could not allow myself to be drafted into the Army.

I considered joining the Navy SEALs or the Army Rangers, but in my heart I knew that I could only be a Marine. I went downtown to talk to a recruiter, not sure if I wanted to go through with it, but the gunnery sergeant there painted such a wonderful picture of how my problem could be solved that I was convinced to sign up. Before I did, the sergeant warned me that the buildup in Vietnam would very likely land me in combat. That was no deterrent to me. I believed that Communism was a latter-day form of slavery, the imposition of which by an outside force the people of South Vietnam were gallantly resisting. I had some misgivings about whether or not it was our business to get involved, but in general I believed what I read in the newspaper.

McLean and Ciantar, half drunk on twenty-five-cent drinks, stumbled through the door and brought me out of my daydreams. The next day we were at the appointed place at the appointed time, my friends still in a fog of cheap booze. As expected, before our lift out arrived, we sat on the hard concrete floor of the hangar for hours past our departure time. Finally, a stubby C-123 churned up to the hangar and lurched to a halt. Still we waited. When we were finally loaded onto the plane, we were strapped to the bulkheads in hammocklike seats, treated like the cargo that had just come off. Then the two smoky piston engines growled loudly, the transport plane jumped off the runway after only a few seconds of taxi time, then went into a steep climb. Like loose bags of potatoes, we swung toward the tail of the plane. The engines were so loud that we had to yell to hear each other. I was concerned that we were traveling without weapons, but laughed at myself when I realized there would be no need for them if the plane went down.

At the end of the bumpy flight, we dropped abruptly into Dong Ha in a steep dive. Compared to the hustle and bustle of Da Nang, Dong Ha was a languid little shantytown. Little plywood shacks lined the runway just as in Da Nang, but that's where the similarity ended. At the end of the runway the charred remains of an F-4 Phantom sat on its belly like a stolen car, stripped and abandoned. There was no organized reception party as in Da Nang; the crew chief of the plane just pointed us toward a dusty little shack that was battalion headquarters.

We picked up our seabags from the oily tarmac and walked toward the big red numbers that were the same as on our orders, 1/4. About a dozen of us crowded into the shack and dropped our bags on the floor, but the clerks there went on about their business without giving us the slightest bit of attention. After a minute or two of waiting to be noticed, Ciantar knocked loudly on the desk of the nearest clerk and said, "Can we get some service here or should we just go home?"

"Why don't you just do that," a clerk sarcastically snapped. A sweaty sergeant interceded and took our travel orders, then had another equally rumpled Marine escort us to a big metal supply shed where we were issued 782 gear (pack, canteen, belts, etc.) and, finally, a rifle. From there a leathery staff sergeant sent half of us to a tent marked Alpha Company and the others to a tent marked Bravo. McLean, Ciantar, and I made sure we stayed together.

The tent was empty, except for about ten cots jammed into one corner. It seemed odd that we should be so closely quartered in such a large tent, but since the Marine Corps owed no debt to common sense, I left the cots where they were. A few minutes later a short, powerfully built sergeant came into the tent and loudly announced that he was our new platoon sergeant. He spelled out his name, "Drumm," as he came around and shook our hands like a politician on the campaign trail. Flashing a smile full of crooked teeth, he sat on an empty cot in the middle of our small group and gave us a quick rundown on his military experience. We paid little attention except for the parts where he spoke of his nine months in Vietnam with a Force Recon unit. This was to be his first experience with a regular line unit. We were very impressed with his service in Force Recon. They were the macho, tough commando types whose main role was long-range reconnaissance, but they were also skilled in counterinsurgency warfare.

Sergeant Drumm gave us a quick and blood-chilling briefing on Operation Prairie, the fight in which the battalion was presently embroiled, then suggested that we go to chow because we were to be used on a detail later in the night. Throughout dinner we speculated about the operation and the nature of the detail we were to work. When we came out of the mess tent, the night had turned pitch-black, darker than any night I had ever experienced. It was so dark that we could hardly see the ground beneath our feet. Guided only by memory, we tripped and stumbled from tent to tent until we reached the one that was ours. Later, when our eyes had become accustomed to the absence of artificial light, Dong Ha would seem as bright as the streets of Las Vegas.

We hurried back to the tent, eagerly anticipating the detail, but as usual we waited. Not until deep into the night did Sergeant Drumm shepherd us over to the airstrip to load and unload helicopters. We quickly tossed food and ammunition aboard outbound choppers. That was easy. The incoming helicopters were very different. Out of medevac (medical evacuation) choppers we unloaded hideously wounded Marines, some screaming, some grotesquely mutilated, and all from the unit to which we were headed. Over and over we rushed our wounded predecessors to a nearby infirmary, many of them barely clinging to life. As bad as that was, it was the silent cargo that was most disturbing. In thick green plastic bags and on blood-soaked stretchers reposed the forever silent, some limp as wet rags and others hard with rigor mortis. Those who survived the Dong Ha infirmary were loaded onto cargo planes for shipment to more sophisticated facilities farther south. As soon as the plane roared off, the helicopters were back with another load. Among the second batch of wounded were brown Oriental eyes, not those of the ARVN (Army of the Republic of Vietnam), but those of the NVA. Only three days in the country and I had already seen the enemy. We were glad to see the helicopters return with cargo bays empty.

McLean complained about the stupidity of using us on such a detail when we would be in the field the following day. Ciantar was conspicuously quiet. As we swabbed coagulated blood and vomit from the helicopters, Ciantar suddenly let out a loud shout and threw down his mop as if he'd come upon a cobra. From underneath a small seat at the back of a helicopter, he'd swept a finger. He stomped off then, and when McLean and I got back to the tent, we found Ciantar lying on his cot, staring into space. Cannons boomed from somewhere on the edge of the base, causing us to speculate on what we thought was a raging battle. Little did we know that the cannon fire was regular H and I (harassment and interdiction). Ciantar interrupted with the announcement that he would not accompany us to the field. We scoffed at his chances of bringing that off, but when he went to the battalion executive officer with news of his culinary background, he was immediately transferred to the battalion officers' mess. McLean and I were disappointed that he decided to opt out, but we understood his decision.

Chapter 3

Late the next morning, our small group joined a group of veteran members of Bravo Company on the backs of trucks headed north to Gio Linh. After the usual hurry and wait, the six-truck convoy rumbled out onto a dusty little pockmarked road misnamed Highway 1. At the front of the convoy was a jeep fitted with a .50 caliber machine gun, and to the rear was a tanklike vehicle mounted with two 40-millimeter guns. Riding past us in the opposite direction on a similar convoy were Marines so thickly covered with red dust that their faces seemed featureless. We rolled down the road at the breakneck speed of twenty-five miles per hour, billowing clouds of dust behind us. Sights along the roadside quickly caused fascination to overcome apprehension. A patchwork of brown and green rice fields was dotted with thatched-roof homes with gleaming whitewashed walls. Black-pajama-clad women walked along the roadside with heavily laden baskets bobbing at the ends of long bamboo poles. My first impression of a real Vietnamese village was not at all the picture of abject poverty that was painted in the American press. The people looked pretty healthy and the countryside looked orderly. I had seen far worse places in Houston. Besides a few begging children, people seemed to pay little attention to our small convoy. Just the same, I kept my rifle pointed out the side of the truck and watched closely for any sign of hostile presences. The population grew thinner the farther north we

traveled, so that by the time we passed the village of Gio
Linh, there were no more civilians in the countryside.
The road ran out at a small hilltop fire support base that
took its name from the last village on the road, Gio Linh.

Instead of driving into the base, the convoy continued
out onto a wide expanse of freshly plowed earth. A strip
of land about five hundred yards wide had been scraped
clean of every twig as far as the eye could see in the
gently rolling hills. We rolled westward past a fleet of
bulldozers that steadily widened the scar in the carpet
of short trees and tall bushes. Finally, after traveling
about two miles over the bumpy causeway, we came to a
halt not far from a small group of Marines standing near
its southern edge. Before the truck drivers could stop
their engines, a loud explosion lifted a geyser of red dirt
about a hundred yards from us. The crackle of gunfire
from the north side of the firebreak sent bullets zinging
overhead in a whistle. So that's what live ammunition
sounds like when it's coming at you, I thought. Amid the
swish-thump of incoming mortars, I tossed out a few
cases of C-rations and tumbled off the truck after
them. The trucks pulled away, headed for Gio Linh at
top speed, but the twin forty duster went toward the
northern edge of the firebreak. I rolled into a shallow
crater already occupied by four other Marines. With the
duster pouring a cascade of red shells before them,
Marines on the north side of the firebreak rushed into the
bush, bringing an abrupt halt to the shooting.

"Any you gents for Bravo Company?" a tall, thin staff
sergeant asked. My affirmative answer brought a clamor
of protest from the other men in the crater.

"Nawh, Sarge, let him come to Alpha," said a big
ebony fellow as I followed the sergeant to a cluster of
new guys near a shallow depression.

"I'll make this quick," the skinny sergeant said, wearing a puzzling smile. "Sorry you wus so rudely greeted,
but this is a good example of working conditions around

here. The main thing we do right now is to protect the bulldozers cutting this firebreak. It's gonna go from the ocean all the way into Laos, so we gonna have work to do for a long time to come. Now, them gents across the river don't care for this little project one bit, so you can expect these little shootin' matches every day. Don't get too anxious, but don't be slow, just watch the people around you. You go hard-chargin' and you might fine yo'self up to yo' asshole in Vietnamese gentlemen."

In the middle of the staff sergeant's speech, Sergeant Drumm came up and introduced himself in the same glad-handed way as when we met him. The skinny staff sergeant's face ignited into a brilliant smile when Sergeant Drumm told him that he was his replacement.

"I didn't expect you for another week," the thin man said, with obvious delight.

After a brief conversation out of earshot, Sergeant Drumm joined the jeep and duster headed back to Gio Linh. A tall, thin braggart named Watkins was placed with McLean and me as we were sent to the third platoon, while Russell and Goethe were sent to the second platoon. Though we'd known him only briefly, McLean and I had hoped for Russell as a companion because his pleasant personality stood so distinctly different from the other two. Goethe was a big soppy blond guy from Idaho who endlessly talked of guns and shooting. Ironically, gun nuts are not very popular in the Marine Corps. Watkins, a tall, honey-colored fellow from Los Angeles, was painfully relentless with fantastic stories of his past accomplishments.

Once assigned, I headed back to the crater to get my pack. Not until then had I actually arrived in Vietnam. The seeming chaos of it all and the management and toleration of it was to characterize everything I was to see for many months to come. Back at the crater, I found that the four guys there had already opened a case of C-rations I'd kicked off the truck. "You a real swiff dude, kickin' the rats off the truck," said a big ebony fellow in a deep baritone voice.

"Yeah, that was some quick thinkin' to get some food off before the trucks left," a smiling Latin fellow said between bites.

I didn't tell them that I hadn't thought of the boxes as food, but rather as cover when I kicked them off the truck.

"We been starvin' for a big ass," the big man remarked as he stuffed a few unopened cans into his shirt. "Big Fifty's my name," he said while extending a huge bear-like hand. "Chambers and Low Rider," the other two said in the briefest pause from their hurried meal. As usual, no one in the Marine Corps used their first names.

When I asked about my pack, Big Fifty lifted it from underneath his feet and tossed it to me as if flipping a coin. "You should try to come to Alpha Company, we got a real good outfit," Low Rider said in a recruiting pitch that puzzled me. Usually, newcomers were treated with disdain until they'd proven themselves, but up here everyone had been so friendly and receptive to new arrivals.

When I got back to Bravo Company, the other guys had already been placed in squads. Sergeant Jackson, the skinny NCO who greeted us, introduced me to Horn, a squad leader who looked and sounded just like Richard Boone. Horn took personal charge of me and readied his squad for the march back to Gio Linh. The raspy-voiced corporal was in charge of eight of the scruffiest Marines I had ever seen. Dirty, unshaven, and with tattered cloth-ing, they looked hardened far beyond the capacities of their young years.

There was no time for introductions as the platoon moved out across the firebreak in a widely dispersed wedge formation. The platoon shifted to a column forma-tion once in the cover of brush just north of the clearing. Horn looked pleased that I knew what to do without

being told. Patrolling is not just walking along. It is carefully coordinating movement that is constantly adjusted
so each man can cover another and all possible concealment can be used.

The air was cool as we weaved through the bush along
the edge of the clearing. The firebreak was to be part of
an anti-infiltration system that would check the southward movement of North Vietnamese troops through
the DMZ. Known as the McNamara Line, it was to be
planted with infrared detectors, acoustic sensors, seismographs, observation towers, fences, and even devices that
could detect urine in the soil. We were supposed to plant
this latter-day Great Wall like farmers planting corn in
Iowa, and all the while the NVA would just sit around
with their thumbs up their rumps. If by some miracle the
system became operational, there was nothing to stop the
NVA from going around it. The McNamara Line needed
thousands of men to do a job that could have been easily
overcome by a detour or a concentrated attack. From the
minds of the best and the brightest came the idea to build
a wall.

The terrain was not all jungle, but rather thick brush
spotted with fields of tall grass. Movement was easy and
visibility was good. We crossed a small tributary to the
Ben Hai River, then started up a small hill. It was then
that I noticed dark stains on the back of Horn's trousers. I
turned to point out the stains to the man behind me and
noticed that his pants were similarly striped. Looking up
the column, I saw that everyone wore red stripes on their
wet pants. I swallowed hard and looked down slowly.
Near the top of the hill we stopped and dropped our
pants, revealing long, slimy, greenish-brown leeches, all
pulsating with purple blood. Horn cautioned me not to
pull away the leeches because their mandibles would stay
in my legs and cause infections. Instead, we sprayed the
disgusting little vermin with insect repellent and sprin-
kled them with salt, sending them falling to the ground in

spouts of watery blood. I could not be as leisurely about the affair as everyone else and sprayed promiscuously with the small bottle of repellent. The leeches were so slimy and disgusting that they made my flesh crawl long after they'd fallen away.

With the fire support base in view, we came down the grassy hill and started south across the firebreak. When we were out in the middle of the wide clearing, three shots rang out. In an instant I was in the dirt with the rifle on my shoulder, but to my great surprise, Horn just waved me on. The platoon continued on its casual march as occasional bullets zipped high overhead. How did they know the bullets were no threat? It was a puzzle to me. The day had been filled with many things that could not be learned in training, but this was most mysterious. I watched Horn for some clue, but found none. I thought that the platoon's recent involvement in heavy fighting would have made them jumpy and trigger happy, but the shots faded away with little notice.

We walked for many hours, until the sun had sunk beneath the craggy purple mountains in the distance, and then formed a defensive circle. There was about a half hour of soft murmurs and the sounds of foxholes being dug. Then came the night of my first patrol, silent but for a stiff wind whistling through the bush. In two-man holes about ten yards apart, we alternated sleep and watch at two-hour intervals. In the hole with me was a droopy-eyed fellow named Olsen who sounded so tired that I worried that he might fall asleep while on watch. I was later to learn that he always sounded like that.

At dawn we stayed in the circle until the growl of two big M-48 tanks broke the morning stillness. A platoon from Alpha Company that surrounded the tanks came into our position. An excited young lieutenant conferred with Sergeant Jackson while other members of the two platoons renewed old acquaintances. Draped over the tanks were six badly wounded enemy soldiers who were gleaned from stacks of straw in a nearby village. Brought near the brink of death by their festering wounds, they shivered severely in the slow drizzle of cold rain. They looked pathetic, with mouths opening and closing like fish gone aground, as they lay motionless except for the violent shaking. It was to their obvious good fortune that they were discovered by the Marines, because none could have survived much longer in their appalling state of mutilation. Equally obvious was the fact that the NVA troops had gotten help from the villagers, but no reprisals were taken.

With the wounded men aboard the tanks and the Alpha platoon headed for Con Thien, we turned eastward just as the mist changed to a torrential downpour. Instantly, the freshly plowed firebreak was turned into a thick red soup and the air was chilled by a stiff wind. All through training I had heard about the blistering heat of equatorial Asia, but no one ever mentioned the chilling effect of prolonged exposure to the rain in contrast with that heat. After a few hours of walking in the downpour, I was shaking as much as the wounded prisoners.

One tank drove out onto what looked like an abandoned rice paddy and quickly became bogged in deep mud. The other tank tried to pull it out, but the more they tried, the deeper it sank. Stacked with wounded NVA and a few Marines, the free tank churned on to Gio Linh while the rest of us formed a defensive circle around the trapped behemoth; without the protection of infantry, the tank was easy prey for the first enemy unit that happened along.

The rain slackened during the night but never completely stopped. I discovered that I could control some of the trembling by relaxing the muscles of my stomach. Amazingly, my mentor, Olsen, could sleep during the driving rain without any sign of discomfort. Pasted with sticky mud and soaked to the bone, for me the night was grand misery.

A single bulldozer arrived from Gio Linh early the next morning. Where the big M-48 had failed to rescue its companion, the much smaller vehicle easily pulled the tank from the quagmire.

We rolled into the little fire support base in late morning just as heavy clouds started to break. Gio Linh was a rough enclosure of bunkers and artillery emplacements encircled by trenches and barbed wire. It was the first line in a chain of fire support bases that stretched from the South China Sea to the Laotian border. Gio Linh, Con Thien, The Rock Pile, Ca Lu, Cam Lo, Khe Sanh, and Lang Vei were bases along the northern part of Quang Tri province that somewhat paralleled Route 9. In Vietnam the fire support base was the front, often deliberately placed in vulnerable areas so as to invite enemy attack, whereupon superior American firepower could be effectively used on concentrated enemy forces. Typically, fire support bases deployed batteries of long-range artillery such as 155mm cannons, shorter-ranged 105mm cannons, and an array of various types of mortars.

Defended by only one company of Marines, Gio Linh was a small fry among fire support bases. It was small, but bristled with an enormous amount of weapons. On the perimeter were .50 caliber machine guns, 40mm dusters, tanks, and recoilless rifles. In the interior of the base were 105mm cannons, 155mm cannons, and the massive 175mm cannons. Attached to the infantry were 81mm and 60mm mortars. The space between the two rings of wire was honeycombed with antipersonnel mines. In short, it was a hard nut to crack, as well it might have been because it was so close to the border that a large North Vietnamese flag could be seen fluttering in the breeze just across the Ben Hai River.

No matter what it looked like, I was glad to see Gio Linh. It was there that I had the first opportunity to meet most of my new companions, and to realize what a peculiar bunch they were. Sergeant Drumm took McLean and me with him as he went around to introduce himself to men of the platoon. Most of the men paid more attention to McLean and me than to their new platoon sergeant. As before, there was none of the hostility that often greeted newcomers. At the end of the tour, I was placed in a bunker under the tutelage of two longtime veterans. Looking at the men who were to teach me how to survive in this most hostile environment, my confidence was deeply shaken.

The sight of Redman and Stupeck was somewhat of a shock. Stupeck, a thickset fellow in cut-off pants and a helmet with a hole in it, was busily scolding Redman when I walked into the bunker. Redman's appearance was appalling. With hair matted in thick brown lumps, clothes so tattered that a rat would not call them home, a three-day beard flaked with something green, and hands speckled with small red blisters, he was easily one of the dirtiest people I had ever seen. Stupeck yelled at him in what I was later to learn was Polish. Since Redman did not speak Polish, it was all the more peculiar. Upon my entry into the dark, damp bunker, this odd couple switched gears and became the most courteous of friends, as if not wanting an outsider to witness a family argument. Stupeck more politely reprimanded his roommate for littering the bunker during his absences. Both had arrived in Vietnam when 1/4 made an amphibious landing in late 1966.

Once settled in, I walked down to the third squad bunkers, where McLean was, and found him in a bunker with two mentors who were as quarrelsome as mine. However, theirs was not the lighthearted argument and feigned anger I'd just witnessed, but genuine animosity. It seemed that one had smoked all the cigarettes of the other while the platoon was out on patrol. McGonacle, a tall, heavy-boned fellow, made no attempt to deny his transgression, but tried only to leave the bunker to escape the scolding. However, Ivers, a hot-tempered North Carolinian, would not let him leave until he was thoroughly berated. It was an odd picture, a small baby-faced kid badgering the big, rough-looking fellow with a stream of curses.

We left them to their argument and went on a tour of the artillery positions. Particularly interesting were the 175mm cannons. With a barrel longer than a telephone pole, the big guns could hurl shells for over twenty-two miles. "Fire in the hole," the gunners would yell before deafening roars of the cannons would shake the whole base.

Back at the bunkers, a circle of men joked about the absurdity of constructing the McNamara Line, saying how three NVA troops in oversized boots would march back and forth over the seismographs to make it seem that a whole division had passed, or that a couple of soldiers and a keg of beer could really run up the numbers on the urine-measuring device. "Was it Bullwinkle or Red Skelton who thought up this plan?" Olsen asked of the chuckling group. "I'm not going out to fight tomorrow, it's too embarrassing," Horn mused. The jocularity faded with the sun, and everyone drifted back to the bunkers. No doubt the planners for the McNamara Line were some very intelligent men who were capable of managing complex multidimensional problems, but management was not the skill most needed.

Chapter 4

Early the next morning the platoon left on a mission to rouse the few remaining civilians from villages north of the base. The construction of the McNamara Line necessitated that all civilians be removed from the area. After walking for only about two miles to the northeast, we came upon the tattered remains of a small village. All but deserted, it was a sorry sight of crumbling mud-brick walls and falling thatch roofs, still inhabited only by a few old people.

We skirted the edge of the village until we came upon an elderly couple who slowly and meticulously stacked household goods onto an oxless cart. They stopped their work as we approached and sat on a pile of roofing timbers. When the old woman went inside a nearby hut, rifle muzzles went up. I thought it was curious that men who had ignored being sniped at should be so wary of these harmless old people. The old woman emerged from the hut with a pot and several tin cups, wearing a smile that I had often seen southern blacks put on for white bosses. She poured a cup of very dark tea and offered it to Ivers, but he waved her away. Olsen did the same. In fear that her hospitality might be completely rejected, I stepped forward and took the cup from the wrinkled old hand. We smiled and nodded to each other, exchanging nonverbal messages of common understanding. "You shouldn't drink that stuff, it'll give you dysentery," Horn warned, but once I'd accepted, I had to drink. What a fool I was. We were there to make refugees of them, and I was concerned about offending their sensibilities.

A pale and nervous lieutenant whom I had never seen came from the rear of the column and started shouting at us and the people in the village. "What the hell is this holdup, get these gooks out of here!" he demanded, then began to shout, *"Ong, di di mao!"* (Roughly translated, "Move it!") He yelled at the old couple, but they kept to their slow, methodical pace, all the while wearing contemptuous smiles. Lieutenant Miller became more agitated as we moved through the village, shouting with greater vigor at every person we saw. All the while, under the guise of keeping the formation moving, Sergeant Drumm went from squad to squad, but it was easy to see that he was trying to keep the platoon from catching the lieutenant's excitement.

Sergeant Drumm's efforts were unnecessary, because the independent-minded members of the platoon paid little attention to their commander. "Moleman is trippin' 'cause he had to come out of his hole," Stupeck explained cynically. Lieutenant Miller was a short-timer, due to be transferred to the rear in just days. He calmed considerably when the last villager disappeared down a path toward Gio Linh. We continued our patrol in a widely arcing route until we were once again back on the firebreak west of the base, and there we set up a defensive line along the northern edge of the clearing.

I asked Horn why we'd stopped there, out in the middle of nowhere, but he could only answer, "We just get map coordinates and go there." After about a half hour of our pondering the question, the mystery was answered when a big CH-54 Sky Crane helicopter thundered in with a tall wooden tower dangling underneath. With the ease of a dragonfly lighting on a water reed, the helicopter set the tower in the middle of the firebreak. The helicopter looked like a giant insect from a science-fiction movie, a large round cockpit at the end of a long thin body, and very long outstretched landing gear underneath. The delicate manner in which the helicopter placed the wooden tower was impressive; however, that impression was not appreciated by me alone.

Not ten seconds after the helicopter roared away, someone shouted, "Incoming!" Mortar rounds swished in and exploded at the foot of the tower, sending hot, sharp metal skipping across the hard ground like flat rocks across a pond. After about ten explosions the barrage lifted. Fortunately, we were far enough away from the tower so no one was hurt except for a fellow who was branded on the arm by a hot piece of metal.

One of the squad leaders, PFC Rogers—experience and personnel shortage made him a squad leader—came over and asked Horn if he thought the joke had gone far enough. "This McNamara Line nonsense has become the worst joke I ever heard." Taking the cue, Horn went to Lieutenant Miller and asked how long we would guard the tower, then came back with word that our job was done. "Well, who's gonna take our place?" the perplexed PFC asked.

On the way back to Gio Linh, Lieutenant Miller called in an artillery mission in the general direction from which the enemy mortars had come, adding to the mood of frustration and disgust; even to newcomers like me it was obvious that too much time had elapsed to have even a low probability of catching the enemy gunners. No sooner were we back in the base than the distant flames of the burning tower lit up the twilight sky. "Maybe they thought the NVA wouldn't notice," Rogers commented sarcastically.

Redman, Stupeck, and I sat on top of our bunker discussing old movies and enjoying the iridescent twinkle of sparks rising from the final embers of the burning tower when I heard a sound that I didn't recognize but instantly identified as dangerous. "Incoming!" the now familiar shout went up as we dove for cover in a trench adjoining the bunker. The explosions of three big rockets sent shock waves quaking through the base and turned the air bitter with cordite.

"Corpsman!" The shout came from somewhere in the distance. Stupeck poked his head out of the bunker, then yelled back for help. Redman waved me out while he took up a defensive position in the gun port. I raced out of the bunker, following Stupeck's footsteps to a place just behind the bunkers of the second platoon. A frightened-looking fellow sat in the dirt pushing at intestines that bulged through a large wound in his abdomen. Beside him lay another fellow, whose leg wounds were obvious but whose injuries were far deeper. Stupeck put his fingers to the fallen man's neck to check for a pulse, then put his ear to the man's mouth to check for breathing. Finding none of the latter, he started mouth-to-mouth with three quick puffs. In the meantime, I was confused as to what to do, unsure if I should take the man's hands away from his abdomen. To my great relief, I was pushed aside by someone who knew exactly what to do. Other men arrived with stretchers and we rushed the wounded to the LZ. Only then did I recognize that the man with the injured leg was Russell. The quick arrival of the medevac helicopter gave me an optimistic feeling for the welfare of the wounded, but that feeling turned out to be a false hope. Though Russell's wounds seemed the lesser of the two, it was he who died soon after arrival at Dong Ha, of a massive brain hemorrhage. No doubt he was taken off the helicopter by some traumatized new guy, just as he himself had done only a few days earlier.

The following day we were headed for the tower, or, rather, what was left of it. Two tanks and an Ontos—a small, thinly armored, tracked vehicle with six recoilless rifles—accompanied us in our fast-paced march along the southern edge of the firebreak. The hard training in forced marches back at Camp Pendleton was finally paying off. The tower was not completely destroyed, but was damaged enough to make it a useless pile of timbers.

Roaming the northern edge of the firebreak, one tank searched for a lingering enemy and found just that. In a sudden bolt from the brush, a single NVA soldier fired an RPG at the tank from point-blank range. In an instant the whole platoon opened up on the solitary attacker and riddled him with bullets from head to toe. On command from Sergeant Drumm, Rogers swung his little six-man squad into the brush and swept across our front. When they were at the end of our formation, the whole platoon moved into the brush at a trot. Strung out in a nearly straight line, we opened fire. With my fear suppressed by loud noise and excitement, I fired straight ahead at no particular target, concentrating more on keeping abreast of the rapidly moving line. When the shooting stopped and we headed back to the firebreak, I was very surprised to see Marines dragging two dead NVA soldiers. I had seen nothing but bush. Back at the firebreak, our elation over the enemy kills was dashed by the discovery that we, too, had suffered a casualty. The RPG had struck the tank in the middle of the main turret, bounced off, and exploded against a smaller .50 caliber machine gun turret on top. Unfortunately, the rocket severed most of the small turret and all of the tank commander's head that was inside. Laid outside of the tank was the grisly sight of a headless, blood-spattered corpse.

The whistle of incoming mortar fire sent us diving for cover. The tanks danced around in quick jerking motions, just barely avoiding the explosions. The more agile Ontos whirled around the clearing, easily avoiding the shells. We opened fire again, but had no effect on the bombardment. Unwilling to leave the tanks, Sergeant Drumm had us run from underneath the intermittent shelling. We ran back toward the base for about a half mile, a very effective maneuver, as it turned out. Our senseless mission to inspect the tower ended when we brought the tanks back to Gio Linh, but after dark we were again in the same area as the fallen tower. We dug into the hard clay on the edge of a grassy clearing and silently awaited the approach of the saboteurs who had burned the tower.

Looking out over the moonlit field of grass, my mind kept drifting back to Russell. Like me, he apparently had not recognized the sound of the approaching rockets, and then was a step too late to save himself. I also pondered the death of the man who attacked the tank. He had so many holes in him that he looked like a sieve, but his face wore only a few stripes of red. He must have known that his attack on the tank would be fatal, yet he did it anyway. It reminded me of the Buddhist monks I'd seen on television, sitting quietly while they went up in flames.

I was brought from my dreams by the quietly whispered words from Sergeant Drumm that someone had spotted movement in the grass. I squatted deeper into the hole and strained to see something in the field of waving grass below. "Hold your fire," Olsen cautioned. All of a sudden the first squad let loose with a long burst of fire. "They'll try to come up on the side of the first platoon and run right into us," Olsen warned with eager anticipation, but instead of a swarm of enemy troops, only silence rushed at us. Redman told me that someone had probably been spooked by the waving grass, that what they saw was only a trick of the mind. Whatever the case, the platoon was on the move, and not out into the grassy field as I expected, but in the woods farther west.

At the head of the slow-moving column, Rogers came to a sudden stop just as we entered a stand of small trees. Near the bottom of his leg, the trip wire of a booby trap stretched taught, centimeters from unleashing an almost certain catastrophe. With all the branches, vines, and twigs pulling at our pants legs, it was a near miracle that he was somehow able to discriminate the wire from all the other things, and then have the quickness and presence of mind to react appropriately. It was an escape Houdini could admire, yet Rogers was not in the least bit unnerved. He calmly traced the wire to a tree and happily announced the discovery of a grenade.

His skills were impressive, but since I was certain that I would never be able to duplicate them, the discovery of the booby trap made me nervous. Rogers wanted to lead us around the grenade, but Sergeant Drumm was apparently as impressed as I, and decided we would go back to our previous position, to await daylight before continuing the patrol. Instead of skirting the tree line, we went straight across the grassy field, a dangerous thing to do even under the cover of darkness; however, that route offered quick passage and few opportunities for booby traps. We could have retraced the route that brought us there, but that was an absolute sin.

The grassy field was not the exposed position that it appeared. Most of the time the tall elephant grass swayed high above our heads. When we'd nearly crossed the pool of grass and climbed toward the hill on which we were to pass the few hours of darkness left, the platoon came to a sudden stop. Out on point, Finn crawled serpentine into the darkness ahead. The hushed silence and uncertainty equaled fear. My stomach quivered and my muscles went tight. I looked over to Stupeck for reassurance, but the attitude of his body looked like a sprinter awaiting the starting gun. Clearly, something was about to happen. But again, there was no shooting.

Finn came back and led us up the hill. At daybreak he went back into the grass and dragged out the blood-drenched body of a dead Vietnamese man. I was impressed that Finn could have seen the prostrate body in the tall grass. The dead man looked so different from the NVA trooper I'd seen on the firebreak, I was reluctant to think of him as a soldier. He was dressed in a black silk shirt and baggy white linen pants. The cone-shaped straw hat of a peasant farmer covered his face. When someone took the hat as a souvenir, the weatherworn face of the dead man showed him to have been about forty, old for a Vietnamese. I never found out what killed the old fellow.

As we prepared to head for the second checkpoint along the patrol route, Sergeant Drumm got a radio message instructing us back to the base. He first wanted to go back to the booby trap to destroy it, but Cy Moe, the radio operator, assured him that he could take care of it. When we were a few hundred yards away, a brief volley of mortar fire bracketed the area of the booby trap.

We dragged into the base dog tired, not so much from the long march and lack of sleep, but from the up-and-down climb on the adrenaline ladder. Just inside the gate, Sergeant Drumm halted us from our drift back to our bunkers and issued plans to improve perimeter defenses. Finn spoke up in a stream of curses, expressing what the rest of us silently felt. Instead of simply barking an order, Sergeant Drumm quelled his protest with a reminder that everyone was tired and by saying he didn't want to lose anyone else the way Russell had died.

The stocky little staff sergeant knew how to handle men, a fact that showed clearly over the next few days of hard work. Laboring under a merciless sun, he cajoled and badgered us as needed to motivate us to complete the adjustments to the perimeter. The biggest motivation, which raised our morale, was that he worked right alongside us, filling sandbags and digging trenches with greater vigor than anyone. The need for greater protection was made more apparent by daily poundings from the big 152mm and 132mm cannons across the river. Like prairie dogs fleeing diving hawks, we scurried for cover before the boom and whistle of incoming shells turned to earthshaking explosions.

Ironically, the backbreaking labor did not dampen the spirits of the platoon; in fact, the men were as jovial as I had seen them. We went about our work, sharing anecdotes about our lives in the World—an appropriate euphemism for the United States. As expected, McLean got around to telling the story of my last date with Carmen, raising the cost from seventy-five to a hundred dollars. The punch line, "and the boy didn't git a whiff of pussy," produced the expected roar of laughter.

Sergeant Drumm showed us a method of stringing wire that would not allow sappers to pull or lift it so they could sneak through. However, the risk involved in laying wire in this way was that it greatly slowed our dash for cover when shells came at the base. Inevitably, enemy guns struck when we were most vulnerable. Struggling from the entanglement of wire at our ankles, we leaped for a nearby trench or just fell to the ground. Three big shells hit close behind us, sending sharp metal whistling through the air. Lying in a bed of sharp metal thorns, our bare-chested platoon sergeant should have looked like a pincushion, but he rose without a scratch. Immediately, he earned the nickname of Sergeant Rock. However, it was Finn who got the most attention. He ignored the danger and just kept on working. When asked to explain his rather odd behavior, Finn pointed out that he was surrounded by barbed wire and far from cover. "If I'm gonna die, I'm gonna die," he flippantly concluded.

When our repairs were completed, we bragged of them to men of the second platoon, and as things went, one brag led to another. The banter somehow turned to comparisons of athletic prowess. The challenge of a football game was soon thrown down to settle the issue. Just about everybody in the U.S. Marine Corps had played on one kind of a football team or another, but we had a guy who'd been a superstar back in his native Detroit. Bonnie was an all-state running back in football, a high-scoring point guard in basketball, and a champion sprinter, so we figured we had a lock on any such contest. A beer can filled with dirt and wrapped in socks became an improvised football, and the game was on.

We started out playing touch, but soon abandoned that for tackle so that a full range of skills could be displayed. Bonnie was as dazzling as his reputation, making opponents miss sure tackles and pulling away from others when he was locked tightly in their grasp. The big surprise was Watkins. Everyone had assumed that his tall tales were just that, but as quarterback he was just as spectacular as Bonnie. However, Bonnie and Watkins were as much in competition with each other as with the second platoon, so after running up a big lead, the offense fell impotent. The second platoon slowly came back. Watkins deliberately held back until the score was close, then threw a long pass. The hard missile hit Olsen right in his skinny chest and sent him tumbling into a trench over the goal line. The resulting cheer was cut short by the boom of incoming artillery. The barrage lasted a bit longer than usual, about a half hour, allowing the sun to sink below the evening sky, adding another page to Watkins's chronicle of grand accomplishments. The fellows in the second platoon lamented that the NVA was on our side and swore revenge, but the opportunity was never again to come.

Chapter 5

Stupeck, Redman, and I further innovated our bunker by changing it from a square to an L shape with two wide ports on each side. We sacrificed a bit of cover for easy access and more sunlight. Some of the fellows thought the changes were errors for which we would soon pay, all the openings providing too many opportunities for shrapnel to find its way into our bunker. "And what if gooks get inside the wire?" some asked, to point out a shortcoming of the large openings. Not long after those warnings, our friends across the river provided opportunity to test the effectiveness of our design. No sooner did the sound of distant cannons reach us than our bunker filled with every Marine in the area, including some of our harshest critics. "Avon calling?" Redman joked to those who had tumbled headlong through our wide ports. Quick to recognize a good thing, soon everyone around the base had enlarged the passageways to their bunkers; however, many of them hedged their bets by keeping dirt-filled ammo boxes handy in case they needed to close the bunker.

A well-constructed bunker was protection against most kinds of artillery, even in cases of direct hits. Sometimes a small perimeter bunker would get caved in or have the top knocked off, but usually the occupants survived. Not even deep-penetrating, delayed-fuse shells were much of a threat; they would pass right through the bunker and explode deep within the ground. Very few people at Gio

Linh were injured by that type of shell. Almost all of the casualties sustained from incoming artillery were people caught in unprotected places when the shells hit. The one exception was the large artillery rocket. A direct hit by a rocket was a sure death. Fortunately, rockets were the most inaccurate kind of enemy fire.

Late one night a few days after the football game, our sector of the line took a direct hit from another kind of weapon. Enemy gunners sneaked close to the base and fired three quick shots from a 75mm recoilless rifle. The line lit up like the Fourth of July. Stupeck fired into our field of fire while Redman and I went into fighting pits alongside the bunker. "Raymond, Raymond"—our code word for corpsman—could be heard from somewhere in our line. The armor-piercing rounds had blasted into one of our bunkers, severely wounded Newton, and ripped Pool Boy's side open from his armpit to his waist, exposing most of his internal organs. Somehow he lived. The enormous firepower thrown out by our sector of the line had silenced the enemy gun in seconds. What was left of the gun and the three suicidal men who fired it was found almost at the edge of the wire.

The next day was business as usual. One platoon returned from a night patrol while many small squads dispersed widely throughout our area of operation. Horn's squad was again back in the now-vacant village to the north, escorting bulldozers that were to plow under the deserted hovels. Once satisfied that the village was empty of people, friendly or not, the bulldozer operators set to work scraping the earth bare. Like most of our heavy equipment, the bulldozers were operated by Army personnel. "Keep an eye on the Doggies"—a derogatory term for Army personnel—Horn cautioned me as I pushed into a comfortable seat inside a hedge on the edge of the deserted village. The squad was spread out so far that no two men had direct contact with each other. After days of long marches and hard work, this was the kind of duty we wanted. I pushed deep into the bushes as the sun rose higher and burned away the last vestige of morning coolness. Enemy shells whizzed high overhead toward a calamitous end inside Gio Linh. Stripped of helmet and flak jacket, I reposed in the shade of the bushes and enjoyed the entertainment provided by the bulldozers.

Three loud shots rang out. One skimmed across the top of a bulldozer and sent both operators simultaneously scrambling for cover underneath their big machines. One of the operators reached back for an M-14, but the other kept hidden. Wearing a disgusted expression, Horn trotted up and told me to stay behind and protect the Doggies while he and the others searched for the sniper. He glanced over at the Army guy with a rifle and further ordered, "Make sure that he doesn't shoot us in the back." He seemed far more concerned about the bulldozer operator than the sniper.

As the squad melted into the bush, Redman was complaining that he'd just started lunch. No one seemed the least bit excited or anxious, but all seemed disgruntled at having their rest disturbed. I was sure that the cavalier attitudes of my comrades would get someone shot. The loudness of the enemy gun said that the sniper was very close. My eyes swept the dense vegetation like a searchlight. I never felt so alone in my life. Every second seemed like hours. They seemed to have been gone for days. Feeling my composure starting to slip, I took a deep breath and came to one knee. Looking for the return of the squad, I was jolted by the sight of a man with a rifle. In the blink of an eye my rifle was on my shoulder and I fired five shots. The sprinting figure tumbled head over heels and landed on his back in the naked earth in front of the half-crumbled hut where he sought refuge. I walked over slowly, but without caution. A Vietnamese man dressed in rough white linen lay on his back looking skyward wearing a great frown, his lips together as if he were about to whistle. Blood gushed from a wound beneath his armpit each time he took a breath. I thought I'd hit him with all five shots, but only one had found the mark. I stood over the desperately wounded man for a moment or two, just watching, perplexed as to what to do next, then ripped open a dressing and pressed it tightly against the bullet hole. Touching him was the last step in my realization that he was probably just a peasant farmer who was angry about getting kicked off his farm. As I contemplated the grimaced face, a sudden loud noise made me jump sky-high. I tripped over my own rifle and fell on the seat of my pants, only to look up and see the other men from the squad. I angrily rebuked them for startling me and went back to my first-aid effort.

"What do you think you're doing?" Wade sarcastically asked. Further angered, I screamed curses at my squad mates. Wearing a little smirk, Horn patted me on the shoulder and said, "There's no rush for a medevac, Gitch, the man is dead." Ivers congratulated me for good shooting and expressed relief that the sniper was dead so that he could get back to his rest. I'd been so absorbed with treating the wound, I hadn't noticed that the man had blown his last breath past still-pursed lips.

"Let me pull your coat," Horn said to me as the others headed back to their resting places. He then pointed out some of the things I had done wrong, such as leaving the rifle within reach of the fallen sniper, and that the squad had approached without my taking notice. While we talked, a very nervous bulldozer operator came over and announced that they were going back to the base. Horn pleaded with him to continue working because without them we would also have to return to the base. The dead man refuted any argument that Horn could mount.

The limp body of the sniper was draped across the front of the bulldozer, his wrists and ankles tied like a freshly bagged deer on the hood of a hunter's car. Once returned, Horn wanted me to make a sit-rep to the company CO, but I vehemently refused, not because I was upset at having killed someone, but because I was very embarrassed about making so many mistakes. "Just tell 'em it was like huntin' cottontail rabbits. We flushed him out of the bush and you dropped him," Ivers offered as a synopsis of the day's unfinished events. Death and injury were the natural currency of war, I thought; that was no concern to me at all. I was much more concerned about doing a good job. That shooting was the first and last of its kind in all my experiences in Vietnam. Most other shootings were done in storms of gunfire where no one could be certain that it was his bullet that caused a casualty. Even if someone was on the end of your gun barrel, you could not be absolutely certain that it was you who shot him.

Sergeant Drumm came to the bunker, ostensibly to complete the sit-rep, but it seemed that his real intention was to see if I had reacted adversely to the killing. He need not have worried; death had been a constant part of my life since early childhood. The members of both my mother's and my father's families had annually fallen like autumn leaves. I'd grown accustomed to death. Just the same, I found it difficult to stay inside the cryptlike bunker and decided to go see what happened to the body of the dead sniper.

A few feet outside the bunker, McLean asked, "Hey, Killer, heard you wasted one?" I immediately and angrily rebuked him for calling me Killer, but just as quickly offered an apology for my thoughtless outburst. While taking a reconciling handshake, my friend pointed out that I still had blood between my fingers.

That statement launched Wade into a loud sermon about how all of us had "blood on our hands." Pointing a short, bony finger in my face, he asked, "Do you think you killed someone today? Well, so did the truck driver who brought you here, so did the little old lady back in Kansas who helped put together your rifle, so did the fat, old cigar-chewing aide to Congressman Dingleberry."

I was taking the speech quite seriously until Rogers interrupted with a Bronx cheer and pointed out that this kind of antiwar posturing was one of Wade's favorite pastimes. It was nothing more than entertainment. Inside the base, he was an antiwar activist, but outside the base he was an efficient and eager killer of Vietnamese. However, the role Wade enjoyed most was that of a person who possessed special insight, someone who had keen deductive reasoning and strong powers of observation. He loved his nickname, the "Gypsy," and cultivated the image by frequently wearing a red bandanna over his thick black hair. His dark eyes and heavy stubble of a beard enhanced the image of omniscience that he so actively pursued.

I had all but forgotten the noonday shooting when I saw Lieutenant Miller headed for the last convoy back to Dong Ha. Among his bundle of goods was the rusty old rifle of the sniper. It was a WWII-vintage Japanese rifle, which made it a valuable souvenir for those interested in such things. Almost like a thief sneaking away from the scene of the crime, our platoon commander unceremoniously boarded the truck without so much as a departing handshake from anyone in the platoon. A few days later, a tall, slim, dark-haired Virginian took his place. Sergeant Drumm took the green lieutenant from bunker to bunker to introduce him to the troops whom he was soon to lead, but half the platoon was out, some detached to Alpha Company, some on squad ambush, and others escorting a convoy to Dong Ha.

There were never enough infantrymen to go around. Lieutenant Burke was surprised and dismayed at the paucity of troops at his disposal. Sergeant Drumm tried to allay his fears by informing him that he could borrow men from other units if he was given some assignment with greater manpower needs than the platoon could handle. The explanation hardly satisfied the new commander.

The critical shortage of grunts limited most of our

work to daytime squad-size patrols and fixed-place night ambushes. No squad in our platoon was greater than eight men, and one had only six. I grew to love the small operations, because they developed the crafts that I needed to become a seasoned field trooper. Map and compass reading, radio techniques, and other such skills were polished, but stealth and bush sense were most developed during those patrols. Also, the self-reliant frame of mind of my fellow squad members tended to rub off.

Others in the platoon were not as happy to work in these small groups, because the enemy moved through the area in large units. It was bad enough that we were much outnumbered in this region, but the NVA could also closely match us in firepower. If we called in the 81mm mortars, they had 85mm recoilless rifles; we had 105mm artillery, they had 100mm; if we called in 155mm cannons, they called in 130mm cannons. Even our 175mm monsters, they could match with 152mm guns. Our trump card was airpower. This loose parity in heavy weapons enabled the NVA to attack in large formations and to hold and defend territory for long periods of time, all of which gave a very conventional quality to war along the DMZ. However, an examination of hardware does little to explain the fighting quality of the North Vietnamese Army. Bold strategies, enormous discipline, and unwavering determination were among their most potent weapons. All the virtues that were supposed to wear American labels were in North Vietnamese hands, especially creativity.

On the first day of May we got a lesson in Vietnamese boldness when a small group of uniformed enemy soldiers mingled with a group of civilians who had returned to a graveyard to dig out their family remains. The civilians were shepherded along a little dirt road just outside the perimeter. Unable to contain their fear any further, the hapless villagers bolted in panic. "Gooks in the wire!"

came the screamed alarm that sent everyone to fighting positions. Like everyone else, I rushed to my fighting position and pointed my rifle out into a predetermined field of fire, but all I saw were frantically scrambling villagers dashing among abandoned pots of dead. Stupeck fired a short burst of machine-gun fire high into the air and many of the villagers fell to the ground. Up and down the line the rest did the same. The scene on the road was utter chaos; some people lay on the ground, some ran in all directions, some clung to each other in tight balls of fear, and all seemed to cry out for salvation.

Amid the hysteria, four NVA troops separated themselves from the civilians and dashed for cover in the nearby brush. Twin forties splashed the brush with a shower of red sparks, and was soon followed by loudly shouted orders to "cease fire." A search party was out even before the smoke had cleared, but they moved with considerable caution in spite of being right on the edge of the base. Like the rest of us, they could not believe the intrepid four had come alone, exposing themselves in broad daylight and practically walking through the front gate.

People scurried down the road, leaving behind a few others still sprawled in the dust. Over the lifeless body of a skinny old man a young woman kneeled, wailing an awful cry and pulling at her hair as she flung her head back and forth. Her sorrowful howls and the pathetic sight of her stroking the tear-drenched face of the old man pulled a few of us from our bunkers to listen to her mournful announcement. The cacophony of combat activity could not seem to cover her cries.

I walked over to a place between the bunkers where a few fellows stood and asked Wade about the progress of the search party, but he instinctively knew that I was there to see the woman. "They all seem to be able to make that noise," he said of the crying woman, and the others all agreed.

"No matter how many times I hear it, it still goes down to my bones," Horn said.

What a bunch of weirdos, I thought, so moved by the accidental death of an old man when they had so recently treated the dead sniper like a piece of meat.

"That's my gook out there," Goethe said as he walked up from behind, craning his neck to get a better look.

"You mean you shot the old man?" Horn asked in astonishment.

With pride in his voice Goethe answered, "I cut him off that bicycle just as he was comin'—"

His eyes glowing red with anger, Horn cut Goethe short with two quickly delivered blows to the face. Goethe fell to the ground and Horn stomped and kicked him with great vigor. All the while, the group watched impassively, seemingly taking little note of the personal assault.

Bonnie finally pulled Horn away. "You won't get another pair of boots for two months, don't wear those out," he said.

They walked away, a signal to the rest of us to do the same. Doc Hewitt and I turned back, drawn by a loud scream. The still-groggy Goethe had tried to get to his feet, but fell over in pain. Doc Hewitt immediately discovered that his pelvis was broken, but instead of treating him, he went to get Horn from the nearby bunker.

"Get a medevac," Horn instructed the corpsman, and told Bonnie to get his rifle from the bunker. I got a stretcher as Goethe pleaded for his life. "You'd be dead if I wanted to kill you, you slimy geek," Horn responded. Just the same, I worried for Goethe's safety as Horn and Bonnie roughly threw him onto the stretcher and headed for the LZ. I headed back toward my bunker, but couldn't make it all the way. Instead, I ran to the LZ, where I found Bonnie with a rifle pointed between Goethe's legs.

A big 175mm cannon went off and so did the rifle. Thinking that they had killed Goethe, I stopped.

However, I could not avoid the issue. I drew close in time to hear Horn say, "I could put KIA on this card just as easily as WIA." Goethe was more than happy to leave as a casualty of whatever combat story he could concoct. With his short career in our platoon ended, Goethe was lifted away to a hospital as a heroic victim of enemy engagement. This very bizarre day ended when the search party returned with the bodies of two dead NVA soldiers.

During the night, a rumor swept around the line that the enemy soldiers had taken such a risk in preparation for a ground attack soon to come. Inside our bunker, Stupeck nervously cleaned and straightened things that did not need cleaning or straightening. I countered the rumor with the hypothesis that the intrepid four were opportunists who took advantage of a passing crowd of civilians. Stupeck relaxed.

Redman took the point of view of the rumor, and said that if I was right, the NVA could have stopped the civilians farther down the road and asked all the questions they wanted to ask to find out the layout of the base. Stupeck again got nervous.

"They didn't know those people any more than we did," I said. If they wanted reliable information about the base, such as gun placements and radio equipment, they would have to look themselves. Much to Stupeck's relief, Watkins came for a visit and to grace us with stories that took us far from Vietnam.

At daybreak the next morning, the first platoon sent a squad to intercept a big crowd of civilians marching up Highway 1. The little squad stood in the middle of the road, but the mob just went around them. Even when shots were fired into the air, they would not stop. Sergeant Drumm hurriedly hustled our platoon on the road to block the path of the very determined people. Amazingly, the intention of the people was to return to their old homes. Bombed, shot, and brutalized daily, these people still wanted to return to their land. The grandest irony was that the land was of such poor quality that it afforded only the barest living. The motley mob sat in the road while ARVN soldiers vainly tried to persuade them to leave. The people were quiet and orderly, but their determination would not be shaken by threats or bribes. Only when a landowner from Quang Tri City told them that the fields they rented had been sold did the mob start to break up and drift away.

Later that evening, an intelligence report of an NVA battalion headed our way put the base on full alert and pulled in all troops except for a few who were sent out on listening posts. The report was confirmation of the previous night's rumor. Sergeant Drumm and Lieutenant Burke came around to make sure we were prepared for the most severe eventuality and to pass along the small amount of information about the enemy that they possessed. When the lieutenant said the anticipated enemy was from the 385th Regiment of the 324B Division, even the sleepy-eyed Redman paid close attention. Our battalion had fought a series of bloody battles with that group only a few months earlier.

Of course, it was my turn to go out on listening post. Because of the strong possibility of attack, Sergeant Drumm held a special briefing with the three of us who were to go on the LP. Instructions were very precise, and Sergeant Drumm was especially emphatic about the position we were to take. Routes to and from the LP were very strict. All the radio procedures were nonverbal, clicks of the handset to mean different things. Ivers, Olsen, and I moved out through the darkness, very careful to stay along the path prescribed. Ivers, the team leader, took the point, and I brought up the rear with the radio. The heavy cloud cover broke and shafts of bright moonlight bathed the thickets as we moved stealthily along the way. We moved so smoothly through territory very familiar to us that we did not so much as interrupt the songs of insects and night creatures. At the edge of what remained of the village, we were surprised and somewhat worried by a row of holes that went right across our position. Obedient to our instructions, we took up position exactly as ordered, in spite of our worries that the holes might soon be occupied by people we did not like.

Soon after we took position, the air was thumped by the familiar sound of a small mortar tube that sent shells into Gio Linh. I winced at the sound, but all the shells flew high overhead and crashed into the base. While he marveled at the number of rounds the enemy could put in the air, Olsen thought it was only a 60mm, not worth breaking radio silence. To our surprise, the company commander came over the radio and asked for the location of the enemy mortar tube. I relayed Olsen's calculations, and minutes later 105mm rounds impacted in an area to our northwest. The enemy mortar fell silent. A few minutes later, the big guns across the river opened up, apparently prompted by the flashes of our 105mm's. Of course, our big guns responded, and a full-scale artillery duel ensued.

At first I was happy to be out of Gio Linh as the heavy shells whistled past, headed for a fiery end inside the base, but it also occurred to me that the shelling was the prelude to the start of a ground attack. Then the shells started to fall short of the base, crashing uncomfortably close to our position. A big shell fell in front of us in a thunderous explosion that left my ears ringing, then another hit behind and showered us with dirt. "Get out of here!" Ivers yelled as he dashed for cover behind the wall of a half-crushed pagoda. In the midst of the frightful explosions, we covered the short distance to the wall in a flash and cringed there in fear until the barrage was over.

With neither side able to suppress the other, the artillery duel soon quieted to an occasional round of H&I. We moved back to our original position, but instead of taking the direct route across the clearing that we covered during the barrage, we moved through the thick brush. We were almost back to the place where we started from when I heard a message that stopped us in our tracks.

"Got movement to your direct front" was the very nervous announcement of the man in the tower inside the base to our platoon CP. Sergeant Drumm's abrupt answer reminded us of the .50 caliber machine gun in the tower. I broke into the transmission and reported that we had moved because of the incoming artillery. Lieutenant Burke told us to stay still, and then asked the tower if he still saw movement.

He answered, "Yes." The company CP broke into the net and asked the man in the tower further questions about the movement he saw. The situation got very confused very fast. No one was sure if the movement was enemy soldiers or us. Ivers took us back to the three small holes that had become one large hole. The guy in the tower went crazy with reports of movement.

"That was us, you jackass!" I whispered emphatically.

"Hold your fire," Lieutenant Burke ordered.

Before the lieutenant could sort out whether the man in the tower saw us or someone else, Ivers stood up and lit his cigarette lighter. "That's our position," he said impatiently. The small lighter seemed as bright as a Roman candle.

In the flash of a second, gunfire erupted from the bush to our left. Muzzle flashes were like a thousand fireflies. Like Olympic sprinters, we were again on the run, bolting from the hole as fast as our legs could take us. Not until we were on the edge of the clearing in front of the base did we stop. I requested permission to enter, but Lieutenant Burke told us to stay where we were. Flares burst overhead and guns from the base blasted the area from which we had just come. Still breathing hard, I turned to Ivers and said, "Well, Stanley, this is another fine mess you've gotten me into!" Crazy as it seemed, we lay there laughing at each other while the shooting raged on.

We passed the night sleeplessly, then moved back into the base at first sunlight. The attack had not come. "Do you think the guys will know what happened?" Ivers asked as we walked through the gate. His question was soon answered; nearly everybody in our squad came out of their bunkers and held cigarette lighters high above their heads.

"Give me your tired, poor, and huddled masses," Rogers said before breaking down with laughter. Ivers, a hot-tempered sort, took the ribbing with a soft, embarrassed smile. He did not have to endure the ridicule very long, because Lieutenant Burke hauled him to the company CP for a meeting to straighten out the confusion that occurred during the night.

Even though we'd been awake all night, we had to go on with our regular housewifely duties, digging out trenches, picking up cigarette butts, doing and undoing, anything but rest. All the while we worked we speculated as to why such a large enemy force had come so close to the base without mounting an attack. The general conclusion was that they had been there to make sure that we did not come out. They were there to protect something more important, such as a large troop movement or the movement of heavy weapons; yet, there we were, cleaning up cigarette butts instead of out beating the bush.

The company gunnery sergeant directed these cleanup chores, the only thing for which the ill-tempered buffoon had talent. As expected, the most miserable tasks were given to the new guys. The big piglike sergeant had a particular dislike for McLean, presumably because he was so well liked by the rest of the troops. McLean and I were assigned the miserable task of burning the shit. This was no euphemism, but the literal means by which feces was disposed. We would go around to all the latrines and pull out the fifty-five-gallon drums that had been cut in half to serve as receptacles. We would then pour in recycled oil over all the shit and set it ablaze. Human waste does not burn very easily; it took considerable stirring and a lot of oil to incinerate a full drum of shit. The sight of a big drum of bubbling purple shit was enough to make a buzzard retch, and the downwind odor was as noxious as tear gas. "You can write home and tell them that we are really stirring up some shit over here," I said to McLean as we shielded ourselves from popping maggots.

We returned to our platoon thoroughly disgusted. After airing our grievance, Redman and Stupeck came to the opinion that the best way for us to restore our dignity was to steal a can of fruit cocktail from the storage tent. We did not have a mess hall at Gio Linh, but canned food was kept on hand for the rare occasions when hot meals could be trucked in from Dong Ha. Fruit cocktail was the most prized of the very rare treats stored there. Just after sundown McLean and I crept out of our bunkers and scurried through the trenches until we came to the supply tent, right next to the CP bunker. Using our best technique to avoid detection, we crawled low and slipped into the dark tent. As soon as we were inside, I heard the distant boom that signaled incoming artillery. Frantically, we scrambled through stacks of boxes in search of the canned delicacy. Just as the first rounds impacted a few yards on the other side of the CP bunker, I found a box labeled "Fruit Cocktail." Reaching in, I tossed one can to McLean and grabbed another as we raced out of the tent and quickly covered the distance back to the bunker.

Still puffing for breath, I quickly forced open the can. Stupeck and Redman huddled close with spoons at the ready. I pulled back the lid, already tasting the scrumptious sweetness of the fruit within. I pulled back in shock. Redman put his face close to the can, sniffed, then fell over backward in a laugh. "These fools almost got blown up for peas and carrots," he howled. We laughed for a long time, then in mock anger I took the other can from McLean and hurled it toward the wire. It struck a mine and set off a loud explosion that sent everyone on our side of the line dashing for fighting positions. We sent word down the line that the mine had exploded errantly, but just the same, Sergeant Drumm came to investigate. We gave him a story that he did not believe, but he just told us to "put a cover on that shit."

Richard A. Guidry

Chapter 6

In the following week we pushed our patrols farther and farther west, until we overlapped the eastward movement of Alpha Company patrols. Though we ventured deep into enemy-infested territory, there was very little contact with the enemy. Even the enemy cannons grew quiet. The ever-worrying troops even took the lull badly, speculating that the absence of hostilities was due to the enemy's hoarding his resources for something big.

One evening at dusk we had a vivid reminder that the enemy was still very much about. A Skyhawk (small attack aircraft) hit targets just across the river. We watched the small jet repeatedly dive on an unseen target, but when it turned to head toward the sea, the bright flame of some kind of missile followed. The plane pulled up, banked, then dove toward the ground, but the missile stayed right with it. As the plane dove toward Gio Linh, the missile seemed to lock on and go into second gear. In an instant it caught up with the plane and turned them both into a big ball of orange flames that streaked across the sky like a dying meteor. We looked on, sharing some of the horror that the pilot must have felt as the stricken plane plunged to earth about a hundred yards in front of the base. As expected, Sergeant Drumm came around with word for us to saddle up, and soon the whole platoon was out to investigate the crash. Even with morning sunlight, we did not find the pilot's body. The plane had all but disappeared; few pieces larger than a phone book were found among the scorched bushes. The on-board ammunition must have blown it apart.

The downing of the plane accelerated rumors of a big attack to come, exacerbating Stupeck's already nervous condition. With every passing hour he thought of some new hazard that had to be addressed. As usual, Redman got the greatest entertainment from Stupeck's distress and prompted him to even more manic behavior with lurid stories of how the Viet Minh took Dien Bien Phu. "They dug tunnels right into the heart of the base and came surging out of the ground like thousands of hungry locusts, devouring everything in their path." He just loved to play mind games on Stupeck.

When Redman convinced Stupeck to press his ear to the floor to listen for emerging tunnels, I interceded. "No, I'm not going to let you stand him on his head. He's just rattling your cage," I explained to my excitable friend, but to no avail. Just as Stupeck calmed himself, a big artillery shell crashed into the center of the base, and once again Stupeck stacked flares, unpacked grenades, checked ammo, and so on. Like Redman, I settled down to get some sleep, but noticed the barrage did not lift after the customary three or four rounds. The shells kept coming, their thunder matching the response of our guns. The incoming shells got so intense that not all of our guns could fire at once.

The 175mm guns just behind our bunker fired with such force that it seemed our teeth would shake right out of our heads. Smoke and dust wafted into the bunker through the large hatchway, but Stupeck's nervous planning enabled us to close the opening with ammo boxes. The heavy bombardment was surely the prelude to a ground attack. Even as the artillery still impacted on the base, small-arms fire began to pepper the western side of the line. The shells came like never before, long strings of twenty and thirty at a time that went deep into the night. The bombardment finally ended with a barrage so intense that the shock wave knocked me to the floor. For the attack that was sure to come, I rushed out to the fighting pit attached to the bunker. Again small-arms fire came at the base from the west.

Someone popped a hand flare that washed our sector of the line in bright yellow light. The view in front of us was a shocking moonscape of craters and broken wire. The wire that we had so laboriously strung was scattered like pieces of broken spaghetti. It looked more like the Sommes than Quang Tri. Fascinated by the devastation, I fired another flare. A few yards to the right, Rogers and Finn frantically pulled sandbags from a crushed bunker. I jumped back into the bunker and called for help, but Stupeck told Redman and me to hold the position in case of an attack. Then he ran to help with the rescue. Just as he got there, another big shell whistled in and the whole group disappeared in a cloud of dust. In a panic, I started to rush out of the bunker. Two more shells sent up thunderous explosions.

When the dust cleared, I was much relieved to see the rescuers crawl out of the rubble and renew their efforts. Again the night air crackled with the sound of small-arms fire as the west side of the line exchanged fire with enemy troops just beyond what was left of the wire. Sergeant Drumm came rushing into the bunker and was almost shot by Redman. With no time to be frightened, he told us that the second platoon was under attack and quickly reiterated our field of fire and fallback position. Stupeck came back to the bunker with the bad news that Sunny had lost both of his legs and Olsen had been hit in the neck.

Remember what to do and stay calm, I told myself, but my stomach was jumping up and down. What remained of the night passed quickly with us tensely peering over our rifles for an attack that did not come.

We came out of the bunkers to look upon the destruction of our base, but the tall column of black smoke in the western sky told us that our base had not suffered the worst of the night. A ground attack had indeed come, not at us, but at our friends seven miles away at Con Thien. Looking at the rising smoke, it all came clear to me. The four NVA who had come so close to the base had probably done so to collect information that would decide which base to attack, Con Thien or Gio Linh. The small attack on the second platoon was just enough to keep us bottled up inside the base instead of going to the aid of Con Thien.

"Saddle up," came the shouts of the squad leaders after they met with Lieutenant Burke. The word was that we were going to Con Thien and we had to get there in a hurry, which meant that we had to take the very vulnerable route along the firebreak. Both sides of the firebreak were to be blasted with artillery while we headed for Con Thien as straight and fast as we could.

Cy Moe, the radio operator, was gone, so Sergeant Drumm gave me the job of adjusting the artillery. I was acutely aware that the lives of the platoon could depend on how well I did my job. Horn gave me a map with preplotted targets and coordinates written under them. All I had to do was call for the right guns at the right time and adjust. With tanks and Ontos between two columns of troops, the platoon moved out in a very fast forced march. Our speed immediately rendered the preplotted coordinates useless. Sergeant Drumm gave me the first set of coordinates and I called in a mission from the quick-firing 105mm cannons. The shells exploded right on target, and from them I kept the artillery walking the proper distance ahead of us. I had to work continuously to keep ahead of the fast-moving columns, but the 105s worked beautifully. The switch to 155mm guns slowed everything down. Though these guns had the range and accuracy to follow us all the way into Con Thien, their slow rate of fire, no more than three shells a minute, and short bursting radius, called for a lot of adjustment. Impatient with the slow progress, Lieutenant Burke instructed me to "walk it two klicks out, then cut it."

About a mile from Con Thien we came to a halt and started to dig in right in the middle of the firebreak. The men were perplexed by the strange order, but they had come to trust the green platoon commander even though their instincts told them to move to cover and concealment of the nearby brush. Just the same, Horn came up and momentarily switched my radio from the artillery net to the company net. A few minutes of eavesdropping on communication between Lieutenant Burke and the Alpha Company CP gave us the reason for our abrupt halt. The tanks and Ontos cut loose with a wicked barrage into a stand of trees about three hundred yards to our south front. Three or four NVA soldiers dashed out onto the firebreak in a panic. In an instant they were cut down by our gunfire.

"Get some VT over those trees," Sergeant Drumm yelled to me. Though the delivery of the 155s was slow, variably timed shells exploded over the trees as one squad shifted into the bush. Without orders, I lifted the artillery. The platoon moved forward behind the protective fire of .50 caliber machine-gun fire from both tanks. Through the holes blasted by the 90mm tank guns, we could see bunkers beneath the trees. Lieutenant Burke pulled the platoon back and had the tanks again blast the tree line. While the tanks fired, Sergeant Drumm got us ready. The guns stopped and we rushed to the edge of the trees, firing promiscuously at no particular targets. Beneath the trees was a staging camp from which the enemy had launched the attack and to which many had fallen back afterward. However, the resistance we encountered was very light. From behind the protection of one of the tanks that crashed effortlessly through the small trees, we flooded the bunkers with bullets. McCracken swung his squad to one side and got very close to the first line of bunkers, but Lieutenant Burke ordered them back. At the back of the camp another small group of NVA panicked and ran through the trees, quickly disappearing into the bush. Finn and Ivers bolted from cover and chased the fleeing enemy. When everyone else started forward, it was all that Sergeant Drumm and Lieutenant Burke could do to hold them back.

The fleeing enemy troops headed for the squad that Lieutenant Burke had first placed in the bush. When Lieutenant Burke called for a cease-fire, all was quiet except for the echo of faraway shots near Con Thien. We moved cautiously among the bunkers and holes, carefully examining each. Fifteen bodies were pulled from the bunkers, far more than we had expected from the light resistance that opposed us. Lieutenant Burke had us take cover, then ordered Sergeant Drumm to take a couple of men and search for Finn and Ivers. We hoped they hadn't been shot by our own men, but the two of them showed up before anyone could go look for them. Sergeant Drumm chewed them out for their impetuosity. Finn loudly protested that he knew where the squad was, then reported that they had killed two NVA. The fleeing enemy had run right into the squad that Lieutenant Burke had left behind, foresight that we all admired. We killed twenty-six enemy soldiers in the brief encounter, but more important, it cost us only one slightly wounded.

We left the dead where they lay and moved back out onto the firebreak, where we awaited the approach of a platoon from Alpha Company. The lieutenant did not want to risk a linkup in the bush so soon after so much shooting. We waited for a long time before the Alpha platoon showed up. I immediately recognized the lumbering figure who broke into the clearing as that of Big Fifty. He looked the same from a distance, but as he came close, an air of fatigued distress was readily apparent in his wide, white eyes. "Sho glad you dudes caught up to dem slopes, 'cause I never want to see one again," he said with a shake of his head. Wade besieged him with questions about what had happened at Con Thien. Big Fifty was at first hesitant and confused in his response, then he was more lucid than I had ever heard him.

His detailed recollection began at 0245 on May 8, when the base came under a heavy barrage of 82mm mortars. In the midst of their own explosions, NVA sappers sprinted forward and hurled bangalore torpedoes into the wire, blasting large holes in the outer defenses of the perimeter. Yellow and green hand flares in the wire cast a fiendish light on the devilish figures that led the way for more than two battalions of troops that followed closely behind. Under the cover of ferocious fire from the horde of troops behind them, the sappers rushed close and hurled satchel charges against bunkers in the center of the line. Once they were inside the wire, heavy machine guns raked the first line of defense with murderous fire while the sappers tried to knock holes in the weakest places. The sappers set up little red flags to guide the main forces along a particular path that was exposed to very little defensive fire after the initial bunker was knocked out, a benefit of very careful planning and a wealth of knowledge about the base. They poured over the crushed bunkers in a furious tidal wave, then spread out along the backside of other defensive fortifications. However, a few of the bunkers survived that terrible onslaught, slowing the surge long enough for many of the Marines to fall back to secondary defensive positions. In turn, the Marines who escaped the blitz fought with such determination that just a few of them were able to slow the attack even further. On the few remaining bunkers that hampered the assault, the NVA used flame throwers. Long streams of flames splashed over the bunkers, roasting or suffocating the inhabitants inside. But the attacking flamethrower gunners did not do so well themselves. Both were shot dead near the bunkers they attacked, arcing long ribbons of flame across the dark night as they fell. Still, Marines in a few

bunkers on the north side of the base survived and kept
fighting. Marines in one bunker hit with the flamethrower survived by quickly blocking the flames with
ammo boxes and pressing their mouths against the floor
to catch the remaining vestiges of air. The main force
pushed into the center of the base while the sappers were
left to deal with the Marines still in the bunkers on the
perimeter.

The main NVA force encountered greater resistance
the deeper they pushed into the base, but fought their
way to the top of the hill in the center of the base. There,
a platoon of Marines counterattacked a force of NVA
four times its size. With a twin 40mm duster and two
M-113 landing vehicles, the small, undermanned platoon
from Alpha Company plowed straight into the heart of
the attacking NVA battalion. A shower of RPG rockets
and machine-gun fire struck at the pell-mell charge of the
suicidal Marines. Rockets smashed into the lightly
armored vehicles and set them ablaze like a torch put to
straw. No Marine would ever ride inside the landing craft
as the designer had intended, but there were crewmen
trapped inside, and they screamed in agony as they
burned to death. While the men of the Alpha Company
platoon sacrificed themselves, Delta Company drove up
one flank of the enemy's front and forced them to veer
from their downhill assault. An Ontos got in a blast for
all six of its 106mm recoilless rifles, but no more. A
single NVA soldier with a satchel charge threw himself
against the little armored vehicle and blew it up in a huge
explosion.

The Delta Company counterattack stalled the enemy
attack on the top of the hill, about halfway through the
base, but it was time that put the most pressure on the
NVA. With sunlight creeping over the horizon, the enemy
started to withdraw. However, getting out of the base was
even more difficult than getting in. They were slowed by
the pressure of Delta Company and the determined sur-

vivors in the perimeter bunkers that the sappers failed to knock out. With first light, precision bombing and reinforcements could trap the NVA in a very vulnerable position. Had they taken the base, they could have stayed and defended it before withdrawing under favorable conditions. The slow pace of withdrawal carried the fighting long past sunrise. Not until 0900 did the attack on Con Thien end.

The terrible night had ended with 44 Marines killed and 110 wounded. The NVA left behind 246 dead. Eight enemy soldiers were captured alive.

Only after hearing that did I realize why our fight with the NVA had been so successful. As usual, the attackers split up into platoons as they withdrew. The group that we ran into was most likely already badly shot up, fatigued, and nearly out of ammunition. Seeking the comfort of his hometown friend, Russell, Big Fifty searched the faces of our platoon, but found only the news that his friend had been killed some days earlier. Tears painted his dark cheeks.

We marched into Con Thien under a blazing hot sun of late afternoon. Except for the litter of enemy corpses not yet picked up, Con Thien did not look as battered as Gio Linh. Because of the loss of 150 men, we expected to take up the defense of Con Thien, but such was not the case. Instead, we continued down the road until we reached Cam Lo, where we boarded trucks for transport to Gio Linh.

We arrived back at the base in a mean, sullen mood, exhausted from miles of walking, of long hours without sleep, and tired from the drain that fighting always brings. The base was a mess, turned to a junkyard by the 1,200 rounds that pounded it the previous night. We had passed within minutes of the rest and luxury that Dong Ha offered, only to face the long hours of hard labor that were needed to get Gio Linh back in shape. Though the base had been wrecked, only two were killed and ten wounded in the big barrage, the same as a quite ordinary day. Without the slightest rest, our platoon was immediately put to work digging trenches, stringing wire, rebuilding bunkers, interrupted only by assignments to listening posts. When, deep in the night, we had our section of the line in pretty good shape, the base was placed on half watch as a precaution against possible attack when we were in such a state of disarray. After being awake for more than twenty-four hours, no one in the platoon got more than four hours' sleep that night.

All week we worked on the reconstruction of the base while carrying out the same number of patrols and ambushes. We pulled the claymores in a little closer, added drums of napalm, but everything else changed very little.

Chapter 7

The biggest change in the platoon after our return from Con Thien was the deeply bitter and cynical attitudes directed toward our leadership. Far beyond the regular griping of all soldiers, the bitterness and hatred expressed a feeling that the war could not be won. Along the DMZ the war was not the provincial, almost private, affair that it was in so many other parts of the country. The great war was easy to see, the failures were easy to see, the fact that those failures fell upon us was easy to see. Scuttlebutt among the troops had for days predicted a major attack, but nothing came to us through official channels. We were fighting the NVA and our own leadership, and both seemed equally determined to kill us. Con Thien had been saved by the fighting skills and determination of the end of the decision chain. Our leaders had no strategy beyond the absurdity of the McNamara Line, at least none apparent to us, yet so much of our mundane work seemed to be controlled from on high.

Horn complained about the symmetry of the LPs going out at sundown and the OPs going out with each sunrise, but Lieutenant Burke could do nothing to decrease the obvious risk. Such decisions were made at battalion headquarters.

Along the DMZ, where we could very often look over into North Vietnam, the solution to winning the war was easy to see. It was not marching up and down in ineffective search-and-destroy missions, it was not holing up inside fire support bases, nor was it anything as dumb as the McNamara Line. Every private along the DMZ knew that a full-scale invasion of North Vietnam was necessary to win the war. Not until 1978 did I hear General Vernon Walters say the same thing. We also knew what the great cost of such an invasion would be, which in turn caused questions of why such a price should be paid. "After all, North Vietnamese sampans aren't going to sail up the Potomac if we just pack up and go home" is the way Wade put it. The more resentful among us tended to feel that everything we'd previously heard about the war was just bullshit.

Our middle-level leaders, the colonels and majors, the smug technocrats, the arrogant professionals, had not the slightest doubt that they would prevail over an army of primitive rice farmers. These were "deliverymen," people who equated winning with the amount of ordnance that could be delivered onto a given target. It was the Vietnamese who showed the qualities that the Americans were supposed to possess in abundance: their strategies were innovative and their local commanders took the initiative. Our commanders managed and coordinated logistics. Almost all our "leaders" above the company level were the equivalent of logistics officers.

Curtis LeMay bragged that he would "bomb North Vietnam back into the stone ages," but it took ten years just to knock out the Tanh Hoa Bridge. The Vietnamese were wholly uncooperative in having firepower applied to them, and easily avoided the best efforts of our deliverymen. The most powerful air force in the world could only marginally effect events on the ground; in fact, there were times when the U.S. Air Force did not control the air. In early 1967 the Thirteenth Air Force of the Pacific Air Forces had 1,700 aircraft at its disposal, and at least three aircraft carriers from the Seventh Fleet circled Yankee Station. Against these flew a North Vietnamese air force of no more than 250 planes, the bulk of

which were very old MiG-17s. Americans not only had a
great advantage in the number and quality of aircraft, but
also enormously better radar and electronic countermeasures systems than the North Vietnamese. Yet it was
the North Vietnamese who had the right stuff when it
came to defining a mission and developing strategies.
The result was that the war ended with about a two-to-
one kill ratio in favor of Americans in air-to-air combat.
All things considered, strategy and tactics were as important as technology.

Shortly after the attack on Con Thien, aircraft of a different sort struck at Gio Linh, when two big 140mm
rockets exploded on our side of the base. One of the
rockets scored a direct hit on the platoon CP bunker.
Under a sky dark with unusual dry season clouds, we
raced toward a rescue that had almost become routine.
The first man pulled from the rubble was Lieutenant
Burke, so stunned that he could hardly stand, but otherwise unhurt. Cy Moe (a contraction of Cyrus Moore), the
platoon radio operator, sustained superficial cuts on his
arms and neck, just enough to send him to the rear on an
early rotation back to the World. The lieutenant's speech
was more jumbled than the remains of the beaten-in
bunker, so Doc Hewitt sent him to the rear with Cy Moe.
In the lieutenant's absence, Sergeant Drumm would have
to serve as platoon commander, a job that he relished;
since Sergeant Drumm pretty much had his way with the
green lieutenant, our methods of operation stayed very
much the same.

With our patrols growing longer and the weather getting drier, mid-May saw the DMZ fall into one of its rare
quiet spells. Because of the chronic shortage of manpower, our patrols were of no greater size than two
squads, dangerously small for the great distances we covered. To our good fortune, we encountered only a few
ineffectual snipers and an errant mortar attack or two.

Possibly because of the great energy spent during the

first part of the month, the NVA relinquished control of much of the DMZ. The problem with controlling territory along the DMZ was that you controlled only the territory you stood on, and only as long as you stood on it. No amount of air strikes or artillery could control territory; only ground troops could do that. For our platoon, that translated into walking miles and miles day after day through the rolling brush-covered hills along the border. We would walk all day, set up ambush positions at night, then return to the base the following day. It was an especially grueling routine for me, because Sergeant Drumm had drafted me to carry the radio for him, and gung ho as he was, that meant I was out on every other patrol rather than every third patrol. For Sergeant Drumm, the long patrols further eroded the barrier between "lifers" and the troops, because he took more responsibility than he had to, rather than less. The morale of the platoon was very high under his leadership, but the constant work left us tired all the time.

Frequently we linked up with other units while out on the long patrols. That was always a traumatic thing to do. Even though the linkups were made in places where men from one unit could see the other, there was still a chance that we would shoot each other. And if we could see each other, so could any NVA who might be in the area.

Out on a long patrol a few miles east of Con Thien, we linked up with a unit from 1/9. Everyone along the DMZ had heard of the magnificent fighting the Ninth Marines had done in early May. In bloody fighting in the hills north of Khe Sanh, 1/9 attacked a superior number of heavily fortified NVA troops in a classic Marine Corps assault. With no great superiority of firepower, the Marines defeated the North Vietnamese on Hill 881 North. We admired the Ninth Marines greatly, though the bedraggled, little undermanned platoon that met us out on the firebreak hardly matched the heroic image we carried in our heads.

As we traded stories about our respective ends of the DMZ, I heard someone call out, "Richard." Not for a long time had I heard my first name. Halfway around the world from Houston, I bumped into an old neighbor and former classmate. With a jovial smile and warm greeting, Alfred Major was a reminder that life along the DMZ was the artificial condition, that somewhere there were still sidewalks, ice cream sundaes, and evenings at the movies. In only a month or so, the smells, the sounds, the feelings of Quang Tri Province had become my reality, and urban life back home seemed artificial.

"You're such a mess," Alfred said in the soft, controlled tone that was always his.

"You should talk! Looks like you haven't bathed in a month," I replied.

"Make it two."

Alfred was a big guy, and he'd gotten even bigger since I last saw him, which was odd for Vietnam. The heat, the poor food, the hard work, had reduced almost everyone to gaunt-faced and lean frames, but Alfred and I had actually grown. Perhaps the insufferable Houston summers had prepared us for the severe heat. From Alfred, I learned of another of our classmates who was at the nearby base of Ca Lu. Our brief reunion was concluded by orders to move out.

Back at Gio Linh, the long patrols left so few men at the base that the work details and much of the Mickey Mouse bullshit was suspended. Still, we got little sleep. The absence of regular artillery bombardment allowed us to spend more time aboveground. We lounged close to bunkers and trenches like overfed cats and traded stories of our pasts and aspirations for our futures. Sergeant Drumm was really homesick. He wanted to go back to his hometown in upstate New York and work as a recruiter before he retired. He and Redman were always turning over ideas for a small business he could run after he retired from the Marine Corps. Sergeant Drumm was only twenty-nine years old, but already he had twelve years of service behind him. I soon discovered that he enjoyed spending so much time with his charges not simply out of military considerations, but because it also put him in touch with a youthful world that he'd missed. He joined in with all the other guys who took turns listening to a tape of Smokey Robinson that Mac got from his father. After a loud off-key sing-along, Sergeant Drumm blurted, "She sounds great!" Following a chorus of laughter, Bonnie explained Drumm's error to him, which in turn instigated something of a musical debate between him and Wats. The surprise to all of us was the beautiful melodic voice of Cardoluzzi. He was a handsome little owl-eyed fellow from New York who seemed somewhat out of place among the ruffians who made up our platoon. "You got to become a singer," almost everyone would insist. Crazy Finn even sketched a picture of Cardoluzzi and labeled it like a record album.

It was during this quiet time that Sergeant Drumm asked me to become the platoon radio operator. He liked the work I'd done without his direction, but I was very comfortable with my spot on the squad. I also thought I would look very bad in the footsteps of the highly competent Cy Moe. Horn tried to talk me out of taking the job, but admitted I would get promoted faster if I took it. Sergeant Drumm could simply have ordered me into the job, but he made it clear that the decision was mine. I decided to take the position.

My first assignment as a platoon radio operator was one that I'd done many times before: carrying the radio for an OP. Presumably, Sergeant Drumm had sent me on this mundane mission to accustom me to carrying the radio. With Finn as team leader, Mac, Clark, and I marched to a hill about a half a klick from the base. However, when we got to our assigned place, we found it unsuitable because so much of the hill had been laid bare by recent bombing. Finn moved us to the north side of the next hill over. I called in our new position as we settled into a comfortable spot among the tall elephant grass. Sometimes I didn't think Finn was playing with a full deck, because he would temper his belligerence for no one, but when it came to fieldwork, he had his head and ass wired together. He was not a troublemaker so long as he saw abuse as a general condition.

We had reached the OP site when the morning sun was still low in a pale, cloudless sky. To the west was the start of the firebreak, to the south was the base, and a few miles east was the ocean; therefore, most of our attention was concentrated northward. We shed our helmets and flak jackets and sought cover among large boulders scattered among the tall grass. All shade vanished when the murderous sun climbed high in the sky. I ate the spongy blob of white paste that was supposed to be bread, then changed the tape antenna in favor of the whip antenna to decrease the communication problems caused by our position on the downside of an opposing slope.

Just as I completed the change, Finn came toward me in a low crawl. Everything about him told me that something was very wrong. "Gooks on the next hill," he whispered as I slipped my arms into the shoulder straps of the radio.

My blood pressure shot up, but my voice geared down to an unemotional monotone as I relayed the message to the company CP. I got ready to move, but realized that the longer antenna would be more conspicuous and cumbersome, so I hurriedly switched back to the tape antenna in spite of the sacrifice in performance. In half a second I plotted the position of the hill on the map and transmitted its seven-digit coordinates to the company CP. Yet I could not be certain that the message was received, because the reply was so garbled that it could not be understood. A quick change to the platoon frequency produced better reception.

Just as I did that, Finn moved closer to a break in the

carpet of grass and motioned Clark to cover our route of withdrawal over our hill. Slowly and carefully, mindful of the slow swaying of the tall grass, I crawled close to Finn so that he might use the radio to do whatever he thought was best.

There they were, less than a hundred yards away. Three NVA soldiers dressed in khaki pants, olive-green shirts, and big green hats rolled up on the sides to look like cowboy hats. They did not seem the least bit apprehensive or rushed, no matter that a base full of Marines was less than a mile away. They casually cooled themselves and collected water from a bomb crater near the bottom of the hill. You would have thought they were poolside at the Hanoi Hilton rather than in the middle of one of the hottest war zones in the country.

A minute or two passed while Finn weighed the situation. We could just sit quietly and wait for them to go away; that is always an option of the unseen infantryman. But one look into Finn's tightly slanted eyes and I knew that would not be our course. Silently, Finn directed Mac and me each to a different NVA trooper so that we would not shoot at the same man. To Clark he waved a finger across the top of the hill, representing the area he was to cover. I took aim at the casually lounging enemy soldier, his slim body filling the front sight of my rifle like the side of a barn. Suddenly, I could see nothing but the man in front of me; I was concentrating too hard to be frightened. Finn fired and I quickly followed. It looked as if I could not miss, but apparently I did, because the man at whom I fired lifted a rifle and fired back. That was his fatal mistake. He was cut down after getting off only two shots.

The man at whom Finn fired tumbled into water in the bomb crater, discoloring it with mud and blood. I surveyed the brush and grass above the clearing for the third man. Apparently wounded, he climbed toward the top of the hill on hands and knees. Finn fired two shots that sent bits of dirt and cloth sparking from the enemy soldier's back, but still he crawled away.

I called in a sit-rep no sooner than the last NVA soldier was killed. Sergeant Drumm came back with the message for us to check the bodies, but made sure we knew that the order came from the company actual and not him. Finn flew into a rage and took the handset from me. "Three down and no incomin', that's all you need to know, we ain't checkin' no goddamn bodies. If you cain't stand up to the damn captain, I will," he yelled. Sergeant Drumm retorted with just as harshly issued orders, and Finn relented. I was very glad he did, because his loud voice advertised our presence, and after the shooting stopped, I started to get scared. "What choo have to tell 'em 'bout these messed-up uniforms for, now they thinkin' these gooks is somethin' special," Finn snapped at me as he headed down the hill to inspect the bullet-riddled corpses.

With my fears only half swallowed, I walked down the hill along a trail of curses that Finn liberally spread. Suddenly, a rapid clatter of rifle fire sent us diving face first into the short grass at our feet. Wriggling like fish out of water, we made it back to the OP site and returned fire. Fast-moving enemy pith helmets flashed over the opposite ridge as bullets thrashed at the grass like a giant sickle. I fired back in a steady, controlled manner but called in a desperate situation report.

With bullets pelting the ground around us like raindrops in a tropical storm, Finn shouted for us to try to make it to the other side of the hill. He fired full-out automatic while the three of us dashed for the top of the hill. The onrushing NVA troops did not slow down a step in the face of the weak return fire. Mac and I flew over the top of the hill with Clark following closely behind. In wide-eyed shock, we almost ran into four NVA who were moving to come up on our rear. They were no more than twenty-five feet from us when we opened up. Three of them dropped into the grass as we fired, but one hesitated and paid for it with his life. He was so close that I could see the bullet hole just below the hair that draped across his forehead. We ran so fast that we were past him almost before he hit the ground. We made it to the bottom of the hill in a flash, but not before the hard-charging enemy came over the top and took us under fire. As if he had appeared from nowhere, Finn shouted for us to hit the ground and return fire with all we had.

I flipped the selector switch on my M-16 to fully automatic and sprayed indiscriminately up the slope and at the same time called for 60mm mortars on the OP site.

Just as I heard Sergeant Drumm say that "mail is on the way," a single NVA soldier appeared in the grass only twenty feet above us and fired a long burst that raked across the back of Clark's legs. He howled in pain, but our situation was so desperate that we could not stop shooting to help him; one less bullet from our rifles and the NVA would walk on our corpses. With bullets flying everywhere and sinister shapes snaking through the long grass, an NVA soldier, so low to the ground that he was almost crawling, came shooting his way toward us. From off to one side Finn fired at the enemy soldier, who was almost at the end of his rifle barrel. The bullets ripped out his throat and sent him bouncing and thrashing about on the ground before a quick if not painless death. Instantly, Mac and I knew that the spot we were in was no place to be, so we grabbed Clark by the shoulders and dragged him about fifty feet. Some enemy troops were no more than that distance from us. Among the sounds of gunfire was also the chatter of Vietnamese voices, one that even urged us to "Give up! Sava you self." From that, we knew they did not know exactly where we were, they were just hosing down the general area.

Three or four minutes had passed since I'd called for the mortars, an eternity when our deaths were just a trigger-squeeze away. When I reported that we'd reached the bottom of the hill, artillery finally streaked overhead. With us firing away our last rounds of ammunition, I desperately tried to adjust the widely dispersed artillery rounds as close to us as safety would allow. The quake of each explosion was a message of hope that we would survive. However, the enemy was so close to us that I could not bring the shells down on them without destroying ourselves in the process. In a business-as-usual monotone, I mechanically followed prescribed procedure, still used codes and long seven-digit coordinates to focus the artillery onto the top of the hill we'd just evacuated. I just could not allow desperation to seep into my voice.

Finn emptied his last magazine and threw his last grenade. I tossed Clark's rifle to him. He quickly exhausted the ammunition in a long burst, then came to one knee, as if about to charge at the enemy. I saw no fear in his face, only fury. I thought he'd decided to die or had gone mad. Beside me, Mac lay across the back of Clark's legs, trying to slow the bleeding and still shoot at the same time. Then the firing pin clicked on an empty chamber. Clark clasped his hands over his own mouth to keep from screaming when Mac pressed against the large holes in his legs.

Suddenly, I could see them, heads bobbing in the grass no more than twenty-five yards away. Had they known exactly where we were, they would have been right on top of us, but they were off to the left. I fired everything I had. Mac and I grabbed Clark anywhere we could take hold and started a frantic sidestroke crawl to no place in particular. We'd moved away only a few feet before Finn stopped us. We were in such a state of hysteria that we hadn't noticed that the enemy was moving away from us instead of toward us.

Over the radio, Sergeant Drumm told us to hold our position because a squad from the first platoon was headed our way and should make contact within a few minutes. I looked around for some prominent terrain feature that would pinpoint our position, but had to vector from a stand of small trees about a hundred yards away. Clark slipped away into unconsciousness as Mac tied improvised bandages over the ugly wounds.

A few seconds after the artillery lifted, the fast-approaching help called, "After Hours, After Hours, this is Blue Bird. Hold your fire. Moving from the west, call when you see us."

I could not see our would-be rescuers, but the message was a voice from heaven. Where before my voice had been so calm, I answered them with a gush of disorganized directions. Before long we could hear their approach and called to them over the radio. I kept my voice low in case the footsteps we heard were not made by Marines.

Bold as hell, a tall, sweaty-faced Marine with a hawkish glare broke through the weeds to our right. His snarling, dirty face was a beautiful sight. My feeling of relief was short-lived when I found out that our rescuers were only one small, undermanned squad. The lanky leader of the motley little crew asked the direction in which the enemy had fled as if he was going to give chase.

"You just cover us while we get this wounded man outta here," Finn snarled, "you gonna be up to yo' asshole in gooks most ricky tick."

Quickly, we hoisted Clark onto a jerry-rigged stretch of ponchos and headed for the firebreak, because it was closer than the base. A Huey fluttered in from the south almost as we broke from the bush. After we placed Clark on board, I watched the helicopter disappear into the distance and thought back to the detail in which I unloaded dead men on the Dong Ha airstrip. I wondered if Clark would be one of those gray and disfigured corpses.

The short walk back to Gio Linh was filled with fear—not the fear of some anticipated danger, but the amorphous fear brought on by the realization that we'd survived by the slimmest of margins. Mac felt the same way and could much more easily and clearly express the feeling than I. The base somehow looked different, unreal, like a strip mine, even uglier than ever. Just inside the gate, we stopped to watch helicopter gunships stoop on the area we'd just evacuated. While we silently gathered our senses, Doc Hewitt rushed up to give me medical attention, but I explained that the blood on my clothing was not my own.

Most of the platoon was already out searching for the enemy when we got back. I just wanted to hide in my bunker, but Sergeant Onegin escorted us to the company CP for a detailed sit-rep. Busily coordinating the search for the enemy, Captain Ramsey shot questions at us between radio messages. "How many were there? In what direction did they go? What was their last position?"

Every time Finn attempted to answer, he was interrupted by radio traffic. He became more and more irritated, and the captain became more and more irritated in not getting the answers. In truth, we had been so preoccupied with saving our asses that we could answer few of the questions. "Pull your heads out of your asses, you dumb shitbirds," the captain finally yelled.

Finn went totally berserk and screamed in the company commander's face, "We wus almost killed because of yo' dumbass order to check the body, and you callin' us shitbirds . . . ?"

"I'll court-martial your dumb ass!" the captain yelled back. In a reflex, our rifles went to high port. Sergeant Onegin grabbed Finn by the arm and Mac knocked his hand away with the butt of his rifle. Mac and I then pulled Finn to one corner of the big command bunker. I cooled the captain's temper with an explanation that Finn had to abandon all restraint to save us and that he just hadn't had enough time to get his sea legs under him again. The captain grabbed at my explanation eagerly and went back to the questions. Since he insisted, I gave him answers without regard to whether or not they were correct. Abruptly, he told us, "Get out."

Back in the platoon area, we got a far more friendly reception. In fact, Sergeant Drumm later submitted our names for Bronze Stars for what we'd done.

The platoon came back from the search after a quick sweep of the nearby hill. They did not make contact with the NVA, but found nine bodies and a lot of blood trails. At the bottom of the water-filled bomb crater, the bullet-riddled body of one of the NVA troops first killed was shrouded in a crimson haze. Through some mysterious mathematics, the body count that went to Battalion reached fourteen. When I mentioned the discrepancy between the number of reported dead and the number of bodies found, Captain Ramsey explained that the figure was an extrapolation of the total circumstances to show the most accurate figure. "Given the amount of blood trails, the spent ammunition, and the size of the attacking force, fourteen represents the more accurate figure."

"Why don't we just extrapolate the whole damn NVA out of existence and go home," I suggested to my bunker mates.

My satire evaporated when Sergeant Drumm called the squad leaders to his bunker for a briefing. Our fire-fight had confirmed earlier intelligence reports of large enemy units that infiltrated south through the populous coastal plain rather than through the heavily bombed mountains to the west. Papers taken from the dead men in the elephant grass identified them as soldiers of the 812th Regiment of the 324B Division, a group with whom the platoon had fought many times previously.

I was accustomed to the disparaging way in which Ivers and Stupeck spoke about Vietnamese, but even Redman had venomous words for this particular group. "Probably the same slope-headed shitballs we fought at the Three Gates," Redman angrily said as he busily prepared for night patrol on which the whole company was to take part.

In late 1966, Bravo and Alpha companies had engaged a large NVA force at a small village just north of Dong Ha. The Marines attacked the village and cut off every escape route except for one directly toward Dong Ha. Naturally reluctant to withdraw toward a large base, the NVA was shot to pieces by the smaller group of Marines. However, the strategic advantage of the Marines was not fully exploited, because no blocking force was sent from Dong Ha and most of the enemy soldiers broke up into small groups and filtered south. All that was left of the little village was three gates.

The 812th Regiment had a reputation for strict discipline, ferocious attacks, and giving up ground grudgingly. If anything, it was their boldness and reluctance to retreat that sometimes got them into trouble. Although I hadn't slept for more than a day, listening to the guys talk of the friends they lost to this particular enemy gave me energy to prepare for the patrol with extra thoroughness. Back in the squad instead of on the radio, and still shaking from the shooting just a few hours earlier, I loaded my shoulders with extra ammunition. Because the patrol would take us through the territory that the OP had earlier covered, I was on point during the first part. No consideration was given to the fact that I had so narrowly eluded death in the same grasses only a few hours earlier.

Wade was the only person to take note of any emotion other than vengeance or fear. Speaking of the earlier fight, he asked, "Did you like it?"

In fact, there was something in the narrow escape that was very invigorating. Even though Clark had been shot up badly, I had to give an affirmative answer. I never suspected that my grubby little companion could so easily see something that I considered a secret. I thought that I might someday confess this feeling to a priest, but never that I would say it to a fellow grunt. When I asked Wade how he knew how I felt, he simply said, "That's why they call me the 'Gypsy.' "

Going over the same ground in such a short time was risky business that greatly increased our vulnerability to ambush; however, the familiarity enabled us to move quickly and quietly. We were soon back at the grassy hill that was the OP site, but wisely stayed off the ridge. We crossed a series of small hills, then set up a long L-shaped ambush in the brush overlooking a shallow gully. For hours, we sat silently, watching and waiting with guns poised to welcome the enemy that intelligence reports said would come. After many hours of full alert, only wind moved through the brush. Quietly, we moved farther northward and again set up the same kind of ambush. Soon after we were in place on another hill, the cloud cover broke up and let through the bright light of a big moon that sat low in the sky. Across a wide clearing below, the moonlight painted long, shimmering streaks of yellow on a wide, curving river. It could only be the Ben Hai, the border with North Vietnam. I was very impressed.

It seemed so easy to just keep going, but I knew that a very big fight was only a few hundred yards away. As I watched and waited, I found myself hoping that the enemy would come; however, the moon turned green and melted into a pale pink sky without a single shot fired. Our platoon stayed at the ambush site while other parts of the company split up and headed off in different directions. I supposed that we were to cover the rear of our withdrawing companions, but such was not the case. We stayed behind on the chance that the snipers attached to our platoon might have a chance to practice their deadly craft.

Scanning the landscape with powerful binoculars, the spotter in the two-man sniper team searched for targets of opportunity. After a long search, he made a noise like Jimmy Durante, "Hot cha-cha-cha-cha," then pointed his find to the shooter. Along a small dirt path across the river, four people pushed bicycles. "You gonna give me a hand with this or what?" the shooter flippantly asked of his companion as he sighted in through the scope on top of a big Winchester. Almost leisurely, the shooter cranked off a round, quickly cycled the bolt-action rifle, and fired twice more. The spotter fired with an M-14. Four shots rang out in rapid succession. The shooter came to one knee and took the binoculars from the spotter. He looked like a golfer trying to watch a long drive rather than someone who had just ended a human life. In a loud, raucous laugh the shooter said to the spotter, "The bitch skied on you. I told you that you couldn't shoot worth a fart."

"Bullshit," the spotter jokingly protested. "I busted the ho dead in the ass. She musta fell behind a bush or somethin'."

"Nawh! The bitch died for a big ass," the shooter teased.

"So what? Three dead, four shot, I call that a good day's work."

"Hey, man, I hope you don't shoot pool like that, 'cause if you do, I'm gonna clean up on your monkey ass when we get back to the World."

The two men laughed at each other for a moment before the spotter conceded. "That mama-san was quicker than shit. She booked for a big ass."

The banter continued until Watkins pushed between them, stuck his hawk nose in the shooter's face, and ordered, "Cut the bullshit and pack up. We heard enough jaw-jackin'."

The shooter's face went up in flames. "You sellin' wuff tickets, I'm buyin'!"

Instead of backing off, Watkins pushed further. "You pussy! I ain't no rice-totin' mama-san two klicks out!" When it looked as if the two men would go to blows or worse, Sergeant Drumm came over, grabbed Watkins by the back of the collar, and forced him away.

Back at the base I asked Wats why he got so pissed at the snipers. " 'Cause they think they hot shit, but they ain't nothin' but some candyass pooky butts. All that jaw-jackin' lak they did some big shit. It's the easiest thang in the world to shoot somebody who cain't shoot back. That don't take no balls at all, and here these two candyasses runnin' off at the mouf lak they some of the baddest dudes in green. They ain't got a hair on they ass!"

After listening to the tantrum, Redman turned to me and translated, "What Wats means is that he hated to be upstaged."

"Suck on it, mudman," Watkins angrily retorted as he walked away.

Although I admired the shooting skill of the snipers, I, too, was disturbed by the emotional atmosphere that surrounded their kind of killing. It had something of a criminal quality. Those people killed by the snipers probably never even heard the shots that took their lives.

Chapter 8

May, a month that began with such wild and intense action, closed with a whimper. Even the shelling stopped. Far-roaming patrols to the west overlapped with the patrols from Con Thien, but never did anyone make contact with the enemy. Hot days grew even hotter, so we spent more time outside the bunkers when we were inside the base. Even when we were not out marching around Quang Tri Province, there were a lot of Mickey Mouse work projects, anything but rest.

On one such detail, Mac and I replaced the cardboard flooring in the company CP with the tops of wooden artillery crates. We worked very hard and very long, digging and leveling the floor, cutting and patching the wood like laying tiles. When we were finished, Sergeant Onegin came in and ordered us to rip up our work because the other side of the wood was smoother. "I can't believe you dumbasses did this," the bearlike sergeant snarled from behind the butt of an unlighted cigar. Mac explained that the smooth side would crack and splinter as it was walked on, but the sergeant would hear none of it. When he reiterated his order to pull up the floor and do it over, it became clear that the object of the project was punishment for what had happened with Captain Ramsey. I told him that we would come back and finish the job the following day and headed for the hatch. Angered, Onegin hurled a beefy fist into my chest that sent me crashing to my newly placed flooring. In a rage, I grabbed the sergeant's .45 from his waist and pointed it inches from his face. Bug-eyed and slack-jawed, he stumbled backward and fell into a dark corner.

"Shoot him," Mac urged.

The sergeant whispered an apology in a soft girlish voice. The bear had turned to a quivering blob of fear, but I had no sympathy for him; I found him even more repulsive. I pulled back the hammer and waved Mac out of the room. I fully expected the sergeant to surge forward or do something to save his life and thus make me reflexively pull the trigger. But he just put his head down and waited for me to shoot. When I started to plot, I also started to think rather than just act from blind emotion. I dropped the pistol to the floor, but the sergeant was still mumbling for me to put the gun down. Like most blowhards, he was a coward.

I left the bunker knowing there would be no charges brought by Sergeant Onegin, not because he'd struck me or because the only witness was my closest friend; but if he did so, he would have to shed his macho image, and that was something on which his whole life and career were based. From that time forward, Sergeant Onegin avoided me as if I were a leper.

Just outside the bunker, I punched McLean lightly in the chest. "What the hell are you doing, telling me to shoot the man?" I asked.

He smiled as if he did not believe his own words and said, "I guess we did go a little crazy."

In a most forceful way, I told him not to say a word to anyone about what happened.

"He's gonna be all over your ass," Mac warned, but it was he, not I, who suffered the sergeant's revenge.

Maintenance of the base was the sergeant's primary job, so Mac was included on every hard and dirty detail. On one occasion, he ordered Mac to widen a drainage ditch that did not need to be widened, then sat on the top of a hill to enjoy the spectacle. As the squad to which I was attached came in from patrol, the sergeant turned to us, sneering, and sarcastically said, "I think I'll take up the ambush position." He then lay flat on his back and put his hands behind his head.

"Ho Chi Minh was a boy the last time you were out on an ambush," I snapped in return. Startled by my voice, the hulking sergeant gathered the poncho on which he sat, then lumbered away toward the company CP.

"Gitch, you dinky-dao. He'll have you out there bustin' heavies with Mac if you don't shut up," Finn warned. Most of the fellows took my brashness as just so much tightrope walking, but the Gypsy slid close and quietly asked if I was going to kill the sergeant. He was really starting to get on my nerves.

"I don't know what the shit you're talkin' about; he's doggin' Mac, not me," I said angrily and evasively. Inside, I was shaken to think that someone had so easily discovered that I'd almost committed murder.

My reaction to the question pleased Wade and prompted him to pester me further. "So, you've already tried it," he said as he took hold of my shoulder. I knocked his hand away and cursed at him to leave me alone, but not until Horn intervened did he stop badgering me.

The sergeant's harassment came at a particularly bad time, because the platoon was in a period of transition. His departure to a job in Dong Ha did a lot to lift our sagging morale. Slowly, the cover-your-ass attitude we'd developed faded away, and we once again became the active man-hunters that we had been.

On the first platoon-size patrol after the sergeant left, we noticed marks on the side of an old rice paddy dike, a sign that someone had recently moved past. Later that night, we returned to the edge of the rice paddy and set up an ambush along the dike. On the second watch, those asleep were nudged awake with news of movement on the dike. I whispered the news into the radio as the solitary figure drew close along the embankment above us. Redman fired. A single tracer round sliced through one side of the silhouetted figure and out the other, carving a bright red arch across the moonlit sky. The wounded man fell in a heap, a few feet from Stupeck's nose. "One blue robin" was the coded sit-rep I reported as we headed back to the base.

By the time we got back, our prisoner was dead. Olsen complained about his turn to help carry the mortally wounded man, especially since he did not look much like an NVA soldier. Finn and Sergeant Drumm joked about how Stupeck moved backward faster than a crawfish when the wounded man fell off the dike. However, Rodriguez, the machine gunner, was not the least bit amused by the events of the night. It was his job to initiate the shooting, and he was very angry that Redman had usurped his position.

"What did you want me to do, wait till he stepped in my face?" Redman said with his usual nonchalance. Rodriguez made some comment that characterized the dead man as a civilian, but Redman just answered, "Who cares what he was? Some guy walkin' around a free-fire zone in the middle of the night was not out to do the laundry." We did a lot of work at night, but only infrequently made contact during night patrols and ambushes. It took a near head-on collision of the type on the dike for two small groups to find each other.

A few nights after the ambush on the dike, Rogers's squad experienced another head-on collision. In the platoon CP, Mac's muffled voice came on the radio with a report of movement to their direct front. I shook the sergeant awake and reported that "Barf Boy" had movement. Mac started another sit-rep, then suddenly went off the air. The abrupt termination of the message jolted the sleep from Sergeant Drumm. When I could not raise the squad on the radio, Sergeant Drumm quickly passed the word for the platoon to saddle up, but before we were ready to leave, a nervous voice came over the radio. "Took one WIA, comin' in." I rushed down to the bunkers to pass the word, then went to the gate to await the squad's return. After what seemed like a very long wait, figures appeared out of the darkness. "Frank," called out the men near the gate. "Zappa," came back the password. Just behind the point man, Mac draped his arms over the shoulders of Wats and McGonacle.

"You stupid asshole," Doc Hewitt admonished. "Carryin' a wounded man like that. Why didn't you just shoot him yourself?" He then switched his voice to soft, consoling tones as he pulled away Mac's flak jacket to examine the wound in his side. In a near panic, I ran back to the platoon CP to arrange for a medevac, but found that Sergeant Drumm had already done so.

"You'll get to skate awhile," I said in fake humor as my glassy-eyed friend was lifted onto the helicopter.

I arrived back at the platoon CP in the middle of Rogers's report of what had happened. The squad was to move from one ambush position to another at three-hour intervals. On the second move, the squad had apparently set up their ambush. After hearing the crunch of leaves and grass, Rogers heard a metallic ping that he immediately recognized as the prelude to a grenade. He shouted a warning to the rest of the squad and pressed himself against the ground. A grenade thumped to the ground at Mac's feet. With catlike reflexes he kicked it away and rolled in the opposite direction. The explosion that followed sent shards of sharp metal slicing through the brush, one of which cut into Mac's side. The squad opened up with unfocused fire in all directions until Rogers directed fire toward the area from which the grenade had come.

After Rogers completed his report, Doc Hewitt said

that although Mac's external wound was small, he suffered a lot of internal bleeding. A few days later a new replacement brought news that Mac had undergone a successful operation in Dong Ha, then was sent on to a hospital in Da Nang. Although we knew nothing of his condition, at least we knew he was still alive.

"Who is Richard Gitree?" one of the replacements asked.

Before I could answer, McGonacle stepped forward and asked roughly, "Who wants ta know?"

"He my home boy," answered the short, dark fellow with the big smile. I scolded McGonacle for greeting the new man so rudely, then introduced myself.

"You never know, could be somebody come to do you," McGonacle explained without apology.

I shook hands with the new PFC, Charles Tisby, then straightened out the pronunciation of my last name. Tisby was from a small town just south of Houston and had just recently graduated from Prairie View A&M with a degree in chemistry. Stories about how he tried to escape the draft spilled over into others about life back in the World, and soon a crowd gathered to refresh themselves in the reminder that there was a life beyond the war, that home was not a dirty little bunker.

Tisby also brought news that our company might soon leave Gio Linh. For days we had heard rumors that we would turn over the base to the ARVN and head south. To us, that was an outrage. All the blood and work we'd poured into Gio Linh would have been in vain if we handed over the base to the South Vietnamese. Within a week NVA soldiers would be sitting in my bunker, I thought. The area was just too hot for the ARVN to hold if the NVA decided to move the border southward. We might as well have turned over the base to the 324B Division as to the ARVN.

As it turned out, there was some validity to the rumor, but it was not ARVN troops who replaced our company.

Instead, a couple of platoons from 2/3 and 2/9 came up from Dong Ha. The grubby little platoons looked as dirty and disheveled as we, indicating that they had only passed through Dong Ha and were not stationed there. They, too, suffered from the most critical deficiency that plagued all field units: a lack of manpower. It seemed they hardly had enough men to keep up the numerous patrols and ambushes that we conducted to keep enemy activity away from the base.

We boarded the trucks that had brought up the replacements and left without so much as a tip of the hat to Gio Linh. Our minds were too much on the luxuries that awaited in Dong Ha. It had been more than a month since I had a shower, or clean clothes, or a hot meal. And the possibility of having a cool drink was anticipated with the greatest of pleasure. We had received Carling's Black Label beer on a few occasions, at which times I was very popular because I gave my ration away.

Of course, during our departure, Wade had to be different. Standing in the back of a truck, he talked to Gio Linh as if it were a person. "We've been together for so long and have been through so much together," he said with outstretched hands, but Horn just threw something at him and told him to sit down. It was just more melodramatic display on the part of the Gypsy. That was our only ceremony as we abandoned Gio Linh and rumbled down Highway 1 to Dong Ha.

Our sour moods were washed away under the splendor of the hot showers of Dong Ha. The warm water was so soothing, so intoxicating, that we could not let go of it until every drop was exhausted. After weeks with only an occasional bath from our helmets, the shower left me dizzy with pleasure. When the frothy exuberance was finished, in mock surprise, Wats clasped both hands alongside Redman's face and said, "Redman! You're white!"

Food at the mess tent was as delicious as anything prepared at Maxim's, and the canvas cots in the company tents were as soft as feather beds. An unexpected pleasure of Dong Ha was that it gave me my first opportunity to meet and talk with Vietnamese people. Daily, crowds of people came to scavenge through the garbage dump outside the gate, which gave me a chance to get a glimpse of how ordinary Vietnamese went about their daily lives. Most of the people who lived near the base had some knowledge of English, so with patience, a conversation was possible.

People at the dump tended to specialize; a man who collected aluminum cans collected nothing else; a woman who collected wood collected only wood. Most people were very open and talked freely so long as I did not interfere with their work. Most delightful of the people I met that day were two little girls who stood near the gate while their grandmother collected cardboard from the dump. I noticed them standing perilously close to the road as trucks sped by, and I went to shoo them away. They immediately besieged me with pidgin English solicitations for food. I stepped to a nearby tent, where I found a box of C-rations. I gave the box to one of them with instructions to share, but the other put on the saddest face in the world and made a most pitiful request, "You givva me?" I knew I was being conned, but they were so cute and charming that I searched out another box and brought it to them. These two little girls seemed unaffected by the war; they were like precocious children everywhere. I saw Mai and Mili almost every time I passed Dong Ha. Many years later, when I read of the Spring Offensive that rolled over Quang Tri Province in 1972, my first thoughts were of Mai and Mili.

Our stay in Dong Ha was short and sweet, consumed in a raucous farewell to Redman, Olsen, Horn, and Wade, who completed their tours of duty and headed back to the World. We headed south to an unknown destination with our beloved Quang Tri Province at our backs. Even before the McNamara Line, Quang Tri Province was sparsely populated except for a thin bank along the coast. We stopped at a small village in Thau Thien, the province just to the south. Along the banks of a languid, mudbrown river that meandered through the lush green village of Phong Dien, our platoon spread out to protect a bridge that was a part of Highway 1. Again, it was a good vantage point for sight-seeing as well as for guard duty. Traffic along the road and life in the nearby village were fascinating. Children went to school, vendors hawked everything from ice cream to marijuana, people went to and from markets, women sat on the backs of sputtering motor scooters with graceful *ao dai*s fluttering in the breeze. It was fascinating and a wondrous change from the barren isolation of life along the DMZ.

On the first day of our arrival at the bridge, curious children swarmed all over us with giggling requests for food and cigarettes. One little boy about ten years old was more interested in satisfying his curiosity about the United States than a taste for some unusual culinary treat. He sat with me and told me about his village and family, and I told him about big-city life in the USA, our conversation taking a humorous turn when I mentioned something about snow. He had heard of it but regarded it as something of a fantasy. Unlike the little girls at Dong Ha, this little fellow was old beyond his years, but still he was dazzled by stories of freeways, supermarkets, and dating.

By the time the conversation turned to the war, I had expected the little boy to have well-developed opinions, yet I was surprised by the openness and frankness with which he expressed sympathy for the Viet Cong. Either he had gauged me correctly or he was too young to know the danger in his words. I cautioned him against his openness and asked if he would become a VC. Quickly he answered affirmatively, then qualified it with the stipulation that he would do so if he could not go to school. The little man made it clear to me that there was a significant amount of support for the Viet Cong among the people in that region, but that did not interfere with the relaxed and easy rapport we enjoyed.

We were laughing about the first time I drove a car when shots rang out. I pushed my little friend to the ground and grabbed my rifle. Marines in the muddy river splashed ashore. After a few minutes of tense silence, a little boy plunged into the river and emerged with a large snake held high overhead. The all clear was given. The boy was displaying a decapitated serpent, shot by Ivers from high atop the bridge. Everyone, Marines and Vietnamese alike, was impressed by Ivers's marksmanship. When, like everyone else, I took my turn at congratulating Ivers on his excellent shooting, he laughed and confessed that it was only by luck that he hit the serpent. His intention was to frighten the snake and chase the people out of the water. In any case, after the shooting we were forbidden to swim there.

Though refreshing, the dips in the river were not missed very much. The real fun was on the road. Heavy traffic to and from Hue was often brought to a halt by maintenance crews that made repairs on the rusting metal bridge. Unlike the leathery farm girls I'd seen in Quang Tri, many of the young girls who traveled to Hue were quite pretty. Using Vietnamese words and phrases I'd acquired from the boy on the riverbank, I drew the attention of passersby, especially from vehicles loaded with schoolgirls on their way to college. To help get the attention of the travelers, I bought a brightly colored Hawaiian shirt from a roadside vendor. I did not have money, not dollars or piasters, but military scrip was just as acceptable. So there I was, in my one-size-fits-all shirt and rubber sandals, looking like anything but a soldier. My clownish appearance and overly friendly manner drew a reaction from the travelers on the road. Piled onto the top of a rickety old bus that looked like a milk truck, a group of pretty young girls giggled and pointed. The prettiest of them looked more a part of Park Avenue than Vietnam's Highway 1, so I, of course, pointed all my inquiries toward her. She just giggled and covered her mouth until I had used up my Vietnamese vocabulary. It was easy to see that she was curious and wanted to play the game, but was inhibited by the public spectacle that the crowded bus presented. Then we stumbled onto something that allowed at least a modicum of conversation.

"Comment vous appelez-vous?" I asked, and she opened up with a big smile and the kind of look that says "approval" to teenage boys everywhere.

"Tri Binh," she said; then asked questions of me in French that was far better than I could comprehend or duplicate.

I told her that I was from Quang Tri, where I had a small farm. She laughed and turned to her friends, the language insulating her from her less well-educated companions. She asked me to sell her some rice since I was a farmer, to which I replied, "I don't grow rice, I grow flowers. But I won't sell them to you, because they would dic of shame beside the beauty of your face." She flushed with embarrassment, but I was unrelenting. "The loveliest blossom could not match the glow of your cheek." She took my compliment as a schmaltzy come-on, the way any teenage girl would, but then paid me a great compliment; she asked my name. Much to my chagrin, the construction crew cleared the road and traffic again started to move. *"Vous êtes très jolie,"* I shouted to her as the bus lurched forward. Her eyes stayed on me for a very long time and she waved as the bus disappeared around a curve. Across widely differing cultures and an awful war, we had a normal moment.

The relaxed life around Phong Dien brought out the best in our spirits. Tisby bought a cowboy hat from a vendor and started everyone talking with a cowboy twang. It drove Sergeant Drumm crazy, especially since we even talked that way in official communications. For instance, "Mosey on down for some vittles" would be the message I would transmit instead of "Come pick up C-rations."

It was a very pleasant place, in which many of the old salts spent their final days in the field. For a going-away party, Finn bought a case of the contraband beer, Ba Muoi Ba. A big guy named Johnson bought several packs of prerolled marijuana cigarettes that were packaged in the same wrapping as a brand of cigarettes called "Krong Thrip." Their jubilation at starting back for the World was greatly enhanced by the beer and dope. After a chorus of loudly and badly sung songs, the salts turned to making proposed television commercials for their particular brand of marijuana. "You'll get ripped in a zip with just a nip of good ol' Krong Thrip" is one that I remember. They all laughed raucously, but at that moment they would have laughed at just about anything. They got very high, because they were unaccustomed to the effects of marijuana. Only a couple of times before had I seen anyone use marijuana. A few days after I first arrived in the field, a bulldozer uncovered a big cache of hash bricks. A great deal of it was secretly hauled back to the base, then shipped on to the U.S. One of the fellows managed to get a seabag of dope, about a hundred pounds, to his brother back in the World. Drugs had not yet become the problem that they later would and were seldom a part of the life of field troops.

Chapter 9

The platoon headed south from Phong Dien minus some of its most skilled members. The changes left us less tough and independent, but more disciplined. Sights along the road were more the stereotypic notion of the Orient than was Quang Tri Province. Cone-hatted farmers slogged through checkerboard fields of brown and green water behind lumbering black water buffalo. Morning sunlight danced off the gracefully upturned spires of a gleaming white pagoda on the side of an emerald-green forest. The place seemed to beg for quiet.

In just a few miles the bucolic scene changed to the noisy chaos of Hue. Our short convoy trucks stopped at a fragile-looking bridge that stretched over the muddy Perfume River. Traffic could pass in only one direction at a time, because repair crews blocked one side of the bridge. Hue seemed so out of place, so detached from the war. Whitewashed houses, wide boulevards, sidewalks—all were amazing sights. When we started across the bridge, Lane shouted for our attention. There, among the waiting traffic, were three shiny, new Mercedes-Benz automobiles.

"Boss shorts, I'll cop me one of them when I get back to the World," Wats said to no one in particular.

"Then you better keep that damn gun," Bonnie told him, which, of course, sparked hostile banter. I was glad to put Hue behind me; its affluence seemed almost vulgar.

A few miles farther down the road, we rolled into a fire support base called Camp Evans. Refreshed from our stay at Phong Dien, we arrived in very good spirits. But our mood turned very sour when we saw the dilapidated condition of our new homes. While no fire support base could be called attractive, Camp Evans had all the beauty of a strip mine. The ill-constructed defensive perimeter had no secondary positions, no trenches, and numerous gaps in the fields of fire between bunkers. The bunkers were thin shells of slimy, algae-covered sandbags. Every place that was not covered with green slime was covered by fungus. Circling the whole mess was one over-stretched strand of concertina wire. Compared to Gio Linh, the place was a shambles.

"I see where the pigs live, but where is our place?" Sergeant Drumm asked.

Although the place was indeed a dung heap, there was comfort in the thought that such a poorly constructed base could get away with many shortcomings. These bunkers never had to fend off incoming artillery, no one ever tried to breach the thin circle of wire. Clearly, the previous occupants had not expected unwanted guests to suddenly drop in.

I had used less caution when walking through a mine field than when I entered the damp, dingy sump hole to which Stupeck and I were assigned. The floor of the bunker was slick with a carpet of mold and mildew, and the walls were covered with fungi. Stupeck, with his Type A personality, went absolutely crazy. "I'm too short for this shit" was his incessant complaint. I could not be a Redman to him; I was too much like him. It was a relief to get out on patrol and away from the complaints and manic behavior of my roommate. The short-timers were left behind to guard the base, as was the custom.

Most of the patrols were close to the base, except when we provided security for mine sweeps on the road between Hue and Camp Evans. This type of work was unfamiliar to us. We would flank both sides of the road while engineers covered every inch of the road with metal detectors. The snail's-pace trips up and down the road were very different from the fast-moving patrols of Quang Tri Province. The heavy artillery, the big attacks that kept things so tense up north, made the threat of booby traps and snipers seem petty.

All that changed with the thunderous explosion of a 250-pound bomb. On the return trip from a road sweep, an Ontos was struck by the remotely detonated booby trap. We dove to the ground as a ball of orange flames rose skyward. The bomb must have been laced with some kind of incendiary material, because it gave off a tremendous flame. The fiery explosion roasted alive a Marine who rode atop the Ontos. In spite of other explosions, Bonnie and Wats rushed over to the burning vehicle and pulled two badly wounded men from inside. The explosion was immediately fatal for the Marine on top, his body burned as black as charcoal and every bone crushed. I called for a medevac while squads fanned out into the bush on both sides of the road. Splintered bones broke through the dead man's jellylike skin and oozed red flesh as the charred corpse was pulled from the still-hot vehicle. The odor of burned flesh stayed in my nostrils for days.

Even after that awful experience, we did not have a strong visceral reaction to the danger of booby traps. Rodriguez, the machine gunner, tripped a booby-trapped grenade, but the wire triggering the explosion was so tight that it caused him to fall on his face before the grenade went off. The rest of the squad flattened themselves on the ground a fraction of a second after Rod and the explosion that followed. The soft, wet ground absorbed most of the shock and shrapnel of the explosion, and the rest went straight up. Miraculously, no one was hurt. Laughing loudly, Rod displayed a bare foot where the explosion had pulled the sole off one boot. It was clear that his laughter was not at the boot, but at the joy of being alive and in one piece. The whole squad joined him, laughing in the face of death.

Early the same day, a squad from Alpha Company came over a small hill and spotted four VC stacking bags of rice into a large pile beside a mound of straw. They watched the VC make the rice look like a haystack, then opened up with full automatic fire. The VC scattered in four different directions at once, but too late to escape the cloud of bullets that came at them. In a few seconds the Marines covered the hundred yards or so between them and the haystack and found three bullet-riddled VC, then immediately went in search of the fourth. Like sharks in a feeding frenzy, the Marines followed a blood trail until they came upon the wounded VC struggling across a rice paddy. They could have taken him prisoner, but instead, every Marine in the squad emptied his rifle into him.

For another squad from Alpha Company, the hunting was not so good. The point man in the squad patrol stumbled on another small group of VC sitting in a circle eating lunch. The startled point man opened up in a fully automatic spray. Even though he was only about twenty yards from the VC, not a single enemy soldier was struck. The four of them scattered in four different directions, leaving behind food, weapons, and even shoes. In the brief time it took the rest of the squad to come forward, the VC had disappeared into the bush. The squad leader wisely chose not to pursue. The encounter was a disgrace to the entire squad and tainted Alpha Company's reputation as a tough and skillful unit. To come so close, have complete surprise, good field of fire, and come away without a single kill, showed a lack of the tradecraft in which Marines take such great pride.

The work in Thau Thien Province was closer to guerrilla warfare than the kind of fighting we experienced along the DMZ, mainly small, unintentional encounters here and there. The prolonged lack of heavy fighting dulled our skills, but it gave us opportunity to groom the new guys. With all the personnel changes, I shared duties as platoon radio operator with Abbot, and acted as a fire team leader on other occasions. Normally, I worked with Lane's squad in the latter position. On Lane's first patrol as squad leader, I both carried the radio and led a fire team.

While walking among the green, rolling hills far to the southwest of the base, Bonnie spotted five people walking parallel to us on a hill about three hundred yards away. At the wave of Bonnie's hand, we crouched low among the brush and moved toward the black-clad Vietnamese. They were moving fast, but still we closed to within about two hundred yards. I could get only a glimpse of the shadowy figures darting among the brush. Then they were gone.

"Drop a few mortars out front," Lane suggested, to help flush out the quarry. I called in for a mission of 81mm mortars, but the company actual would not shoot the mission because we could not positively identify the people as VC. Bonnie was pissed at the company commander, and at me for not saying we'd been fired upon. He got really crazy and threatened to continue the search alone when Lane ordered us to head back toward the area we were supposed to patrol. Lane reacted with just as much anger, but relented to the more experienced Bonnie.

The minute we started through the brush, I knew that someone would die. Making no effort to conceal ourselves, we jogged toward the hill where we'd last seen the Vietnamese. On that hill, we again spotted the people climbing the next. I kept my rifle pointed forward, sure that the five men would swing around and take us under fire, but they still hadn't seen us. When they crossed a patch of wild pineapples, Bonnie cut loose with a long burst of fire that quickly was imitated by the whole squad. No return fire came toward us, and again the Vietnamese disappeared.

We approached our targets, this time cautiously. We found the bodies of four dead men; the trouble was, the men looked very much like farmers and there was no weapon in sight. "Now what, hotshot?" Lane said to Bonnie with great disgust. Olsen proposed that we cover up the whole thing, but one look at the new guys in the squad and we knew that wasn't possible.

Bigler, the new man in my fire team, confirmed our suspicion that the new guys could not be trusted when he asked, "Are we going to burn for this?" Bonnie and Lane again started to argue.

I took Lane aside and proposed that we explain our tragic error by saying we mistook the hoes they carried for weapons. "Pretty thin, but we'll go with that," Lane decided. Then Captain Ramsey came over the radio and ordered us to bring back the bodies and weapons. Evidence for the prosecution, we thought.

"Wait a minute, do you see any farms around here?" Lane asked. He thought that the men had come to dig up a weapon cache. In our search for hidden weapons, Olsen found the body of the fifth man. More important, he also found the 60mm mortar tube that lay beside the dead man. We were off the hook. Just by accident, Ivers pulled at one of the wild pineapples and the whole plant came out of the ground. Beneath the sweet fruit was a small cache of ammunition. The same was true of many of the other plants in the field. I called in a sit-rep of our discovery and asked for an artillery mission to blow up the field. The mission was denied, and the captain again ordered us to bring back the bodies. But with only eight men in the squad, it was not possible to bring back all the corpses, so we dragged along three as we headed back to the base.

When Lane reported to Captain Ramsey, he was surprised to learn that our company commander was not the least bit concerned about whether or not the dead men were civilians or VC, he just wanted the bodies. As a result, we found ourselves leading the platoon back to the pineapple patch to pick up the corpses left behind. The ghoulish trophies were to beautify the base just in time for a visit by General Cushman. Ironically, our platoon was ordered to keep out of sight because we looked so unpleasant.

In mid-June we left Camp Evans in a westerly march on an operation code-named "Cumberland." We walked along a road that was recently cut through the jungle-covered hills close to the Laotian border. What started as a straight, flat road among low, flat brush soon turned to steep climbs among tall trees and thick jungle. Every place along the twisting road seemed a good place for an ambush. Only a few squads flanked the company as we climbed in the still air beneath the trees. The thick, dark foliage seemed to absorb all sounds except for the chirps and squawks of unseen birds high in the jungle canopy. For the first time we were in a true jungle. It was easy to see why jungle peoples tend to be so spiritual; the place seemed like one supernatural being, every tree and leaf watching for us to make some fatal error. The jungle was a frightful place.

We anxiously rounded each curve in the road in expectation of meeting the whole North Vietnamese Army on the other side. The tension quickly burned out point men, necessitating twice the number of changes as normal. When we stopped, the company moved into the jungle on each side of the road, and I escaped my fear through an appreciation of the wide variety of unusual and attractive plants along the roadside. Leaves of gigantic caladium offered umbrella shades from which the forest could be closely examined. Insects and spiders seemed to increase in size the higher up the mountains we traveled. Large black and yellow spiders hung on thick webs strung among the low branches of thorny trees and bushes. It seemed that every plant was barbed, as mean and truculent as the people who roamed among them. Small, pale flowers hid inconspicuously among the endless hues of green on the forest floor while their larger and more colorful brothers sprang from tree trunks and branches high above.

While admiring a small, thumb-size orchid, I met with a tree leech for the first time, a fascinating little inchworm that moved toward me in a head-to-toe step. What a cute little creature, I thought of the reddish-brown worm, then the repulsive little vermin stabbed its head into my arm. Much to the amusement of my friends, I panicked and stomped the leech into the ground. To my pleasant surprise, the commotion lifted a swarm of tiny yellow butterflies that floated through the trees like a cloud of glittering iridescent snowflakes. At the next stop, a couple of small round-headed monkeys peeked inquisitively around a tree, then disappeared. There was a lot of life in the jungle, but only the smallest creatures could be easily seen.

Around another bend in the road and up another hill, we came upon the vacant base camp called Camp Zamora, named after a kid who took a bullet in the temple when Marines first arrived on the hill some weeks earlier. The camp, terminal point for Operation Cumberland, had been abandoned for weeks prior to our arrival, and we were not sure that it hadn't been occupied by the enemy in the meantime. We approached the base as if ready to attack. Rocketmen came forward and machine gunners were placed in position to cover an assault, while most of the company blended into the forest. A fire team crawled up the road, then scurried low and fast into the base. After a brief wait, the scouts reported that the camp was empty.

Camp Zamora was not a real fire support base, just a clearing in the jungle with a few holes in the ground. We moved through the clearing, cautious of mines and booby traps, and reoccupied Camp Zamora without incident. From our experience with the NVA up north, we had expected to fight our way back into the camp, and were much relieved when all we had to do was to walk in and set up shop.

About an hour behind us on the road, a platoon from Alpha Company clashed with a small group of VC. On point for a squad flanked to one side of the road, Chambers moved laboriously through the thick undergrowth until he found a narrow trail. A small group of VC broke onto the trail at about the same time he did. The VC got off the first shots, but fired in a wild panic. Chambers had already started to move out of the way before the first shot was fired. A quick sidestep and he cut down the VC at the head of a column of four or five men. The VC did a quick about-face and took off down the trail. Another one caught a bullet in the back of the head. The Marines gave chase and shot to death another VC before the remainder scrambled into the jungle. The platoon jauntily marched into the camp after depositing the VC corpses at the head of the road as some kind of totem.

The road was called Route 547 and led to no place but Camp Zamora. The camp had been hacked out of the jungle to provide a platform from which our big cannons could harass traffic on the Ho Chi Minh Trail. Though the jungle was stripped away, the camp still sweltered in summer heat that was made all the more uncomfortable by evaporation from the nearby mass of vegetation and from a small stream that arced around one side of the foot of the hill. When we first arrived, the stream was crystal clear, but in less than a week it was as polluted as the Hudson River. It was a most uncomfortable place, especially for Lieutenant Burke, who was already sick with some mysterious illness. His malaise was expected, but it was Sergeant Drumm's lethargy that surprised us. His vigor and enthusiasm had decreased notably, but it was not illness that slowed him down. He suffered from short-timer's disease. However, we needed his guidance more than ever, because the platoon had been so severely depleted by casualties and the rotation of its most experienced members. The day after we got there, we lost Lieutenant Burke; he was sent to the rear in a delirium, suffering from a bad case of FUO (fever of unknown origin).

Our first patrol was a platoon-size misadventure that noisily crashed through miles of monotonous jungle without seeing the slightest hint of enemy presence. But when we stepped onto the road for the return trip, the VC made it known that they were around. The shooter in our sniper team stepped on a bouncing Betty. The explosion sent him tumbling head over heels while those near him dove for cover. The smoke cleared and we looked to see who was injured and, worse, who was dead. Miraculously, no one was badly hurt, not even the sniper. One man had a few superficial cuts on his face and arms, and the sniper had one heel injured, but neither suffered greatly. A bit farther down the road, a platoon from Charlie Company was ambushed by a small group of VC. Possibly because of the mauling dished out by Chambers and his squad, the VC launched their attack from a range too far away to be effective. From high atop an adjacent hill, the VC harmlessly skipped bullets across the dusty road. The Marines did not shoot back, just continued a watchful march to Camp Zamora. Pretty soon the steamy little hill had just as much manpower as Gio Linh.

We got a lot of new men while at Camp Zamora, replacements for the men who rotated from Phong Dien. Most of the squads were brought up to ten men each; not as many as we should have had, but more than at any time prior. Again I was moved to platoon radio operator. Two new squad leaders were appointed, McNicoles and Wallace. We'd expected Wallace to fill the next squad leader spot, because he had a long time in grade as corporal and a lot of time in-country, but McNicoles had neither. There were many voices of dissent concerning his appointment, but Sergeant Drumm loved McNicoles and was not about to change his mind.

There were a lot of short-timers in the platoon, and Sergeant Drumm wanted to build a core of leadership that would be around a long time, instead of simply appointing the most qualified people. As a short-timer himself, Sergeant Drumm was far less active in the grunt work than when he first joined the platoon, and, in the guise of preparing others to take over new jobs, re-assigned to others many of his field duties. His trepidation was increased by the events of Wallace's first patrol as squad leader.

Returning from a long, hot patrol along the roadside, one of the new guys tripped a booby trap that was placed in a tree. A spray of razor-sharp metal cut two men from head to toe. Stokes, a handsome fellow of eighteen years from Los Angeles, was slashed in so many places that the squad did not have enough bandages to cover all of his wounds. He'd been in Vietnam only two weeks. The other fellow, Banning, had fewer wounds, but was hurt even worse. A large wound in his back left him paralyzed and near death. Back at the base, our new corpsman, Doc White, immobilized Banning on a stretcher before others rushed him to the LZ for a medevac.

Doc White pulled at a large piece of metal that pro-truded from Stokes's cheek, but left it in place when it would not come out easily. Stokes begged Doc White to remove the shrapnel, expressing great fear that he would be badly scarred. Doc White assured him that he "would look as pretty as Gorgeous George in a few weeks." The skinny little corpsman was more concerned that Stokes would die from shock because he'd lost so much blood, and he realized that the wound in Stokes's face would bleed profusely if he pulled out the metal. Only the quick arrival of a medevac helicopter saved both men's lives. Stokes is probably reminded of that terrible day every time he sees his reflection. We never heard from either of them again.

Early the next morning, the Alpha Company platoon headed out on a patrol to make the road safe for the expected traffic of the day. It was a futile task; the road was so twisted and the jungle so thick that a whole company of VC could have been twenty feet away without being seen. When a small three-truck convoy rolled into the base around noon, it also brought along a passenger from the Alpha platoon. "Big Fifty has been hit," someone shouted. I dropped what I was doing and ran toward the trucks, expecting to see the worst. My old friend lay on the hot steel bed of the truck, bloodied, but with a big smile exposing rows of perfect teeth. A sniper's bullet had skimmed across the fleshy part of his muscular back and passed through the upper part of one arm.

"What are you grinning about, don't you know you've been shot?" I asked him while the corpsman patched up his wounds.

He did not answer me directly, but said, "Gitch, baby, every time I see you, something good happens to me." His wounds released him from the tension of shorttimer's pressure; he was sent to the rear a full month ahead of his scheduled rotation date. "Have a good life!" he shouted to me as the trucks pulled away for Phu Bai. Big Fifty made it. Two days later, the rest of the Alpha Company platoon also left the base for good.

Chapter 10

With only a few hours' notice, Bravo Company left Camp Zamora the day after the Alpha platoon was deployed elsewhere. Aboard HU-46 helicopters, we took a bumpy ride back to our beloved Quang Tri Province. During the flight, we speculated that the situation that awaited us must be very hot for us to have been so suddenly snatched away.

The choppers dropped us in the rolling brush-covered hills about three miles east of Con Thien. The air smelled clear; the red dirt beneath my feet was comfortably familiar. We marched in a long zigzag route past Con Thien and on toward Khe Sanh. In two days of almost continual walking, we did not make the slightest contact with the enemy, and soon we were headed back to Con Thien.

Walking patrol is not simply going on a hike. Even when nothing of great consequence happens, patrolling produces tension that comes from the effort expended in reading the environment in as much detail as possible. As you patrol you constantly adjust your path to take advantage of rocks, trees, shadows, etc., to provide cover and concealment so that you can instantly disappear at the slightest sign of trouble. Hand and arm signals were entirely unnecessary, because you stayed in tune with the people around you. You adjusted your field of fire to overlap with those of your fellow squad members so that your assigned area of protection was always covered.

115

Other people depended upon you for their safety and protection, and you depended upon them. As you acquired
experience the constant adjustments and elevation of the
senses became more instinctual, but still the effort was
tiring.

After a night of much-needed rest, we were again on
trucks headed south along Highway 1. The empty faces
of young men made to look old by dirt and fatigue
looked out onto familiar sights past Dong Ha, past Hue,
and once again we walked the long, twisting road back to
Camp Zamora. No one ever told us why we'd been so
suddenly pulled back north. As if following the steps to
an old dance, we again entered the camp on the attack,
and again there was nothing.

After our return from Quang Tri, we were assigned to
longer patrols and a lot more escorts of traffic on the
road. Day by day the steamy, suffocating jungle began to
take its toll. Almost every day someone was stricken with
dysentery, malaria, or some other jungle malady. On
patrol, I slashed my shin on a sharp thorn. Amazingly, the
wound was almost healed by the time we got back to the
base. Doc White said it was bacteria in the mud of a
small stream that we crossed that made the wound heal
so fast. He and I joked about getting rich by putting the
mud in jars and selling it across the country as a pimple
remover. Lane said, "And you could put your picture on
the jar with a caption that says 'You Don't Have to Look
Like This!' " After a patrol along the road a few days
later, the point man for the first platoon could have used a
whole bucket of that mud; a sniper's bullet struck his
helmet where it seemed that the slug should have passed
through his head. But it traveled around the curve of the
helmet and carved a long cut in his scalp, but otherwise
he was all right.

The traffic on the road brought supplies in preparation
for the big guns that were soon to arrive, and because of
it we frequently escorted trucks to and from Camp

Evans. On one such escort I carried the radio for Foit's squad when, about halfway between the bases, the white smoke of an RPG hissed out of the surrounding jungle and slammed into the side of the lead truck.

Suddenly, we were under intense fire. On the left side of the road, unseen VC peppered the trucks with bullets. We jumped off the trucks on the right side of the road and returned fire in the general direction of the enemy. I could not see anyone, not even muzzle flashes. Frantically guessing at our location, I called for artillery on the hill to the left side of the road. Instead of artillery, Wallace came over the radio with news that his squad was heading for the road as fast as they could. A second rocket kicked up a cloud of dust from the roadside and leaf-shrouded enemy troops appeared from nowhere, bounding forward with their guns blazing. Directly across from me a man dashed forward, a big round can underneath his automatic weapon. They were just on the other side of the road, closer than I'd ever been to a living, fighting enemy.

I fired at the man and tried to call in artillery at the same time. My first urge was to escape into the jungle behind us, and I looked to Foit for that directive, but he gave no such order; in fact, he gave no orders at all. I fired very fast without changing my M-16 to fully automatic. While shooting, I found the precise coordinates of the hill across the road and transmitted the information to the company CP. "Fire for effect on YD14407," I said with artificial calmness.

The VC wanted the supplies from the trucks, and with one determined frontal assault they could have had them and slaughtered us all. Fortunately for us, that was not a tactic of first resort for the VC. They took cover along the roadside and laid down withering fire in an attempt to drive us away, but in so doing, they also pinned us down and made escape impossible without taking heavy casualties. During the fight, a VC actually climbed onto the second truck and threw down a few boxes of food, then got away without being shot. My rifle emptied. I threw a grenade and quickly switched to a new magazine. A shower of grenades went over the trucks from our side of the road and drove some of the VC back to the tree line.

Wallace came over the radio with the message that he'd reached the road. A few seconds later a pall of white phosphorus rose from high atop the hill behind the VC position. I started to adjust the rounds down the slope when Wallace came over the radio with news that he and his men were just around the curve in the road. The rounds that closed in on the VC were from 81mm mortars, a notoriously inaccurate tube.

The VC had already started to withdraw when Wallace and his squad reached us and joined the fight. On his orders, I lifted the barrage. Wallace jumped into the second truck and rammed it into the side of the stricken lead truck, forcing it off the road. He decided it was too dangerous for all of us to ride on the remaining two trucks, so only the wounded were placed aboard. Foit drove the lead truck toward Camp Zamora at breakneck speed while the rest of us faded into the jungle on the right side of the road. I called the company CP to arrange for a medevac and give a sit-rep.

Captain Ramsey ordered us to go back to the road and head for the base as fast as possible. He was very angry that we hadn't also boarded the trucks, and chewed out Wallace for his decision not to do so. We thought the order to return via the road was crazy and unnecessarily exposed us to danger, but we obeyed. Someone else must be in trouble, I thought as we trotted noisily away, nervously eyeing the road as we went. The buzz of a bird dog (small observation aircraft) frightened me even more. Worried that the light observation plane might mistake us for enemy troops, I informed Captain Ramsey of its presence, but he only admonished us to move faster.

My chest burned and I gasped for breath as we climbed

the twisting road at a brisk trot. Guided by the bird dog, two F-4 Phantoms swooped low, one after another, and released a string of large bombs on the hill from which the VC had attacked. The thunderous roar reverberated through the mountains with each explosion. It was then clear why the captain wanted us to take the road. Some of the bombs fell so close that Wallace had us take cover along the roadside. After the air strike, we made our way back to the base by way of a route that offered more concealment than the road. We arrived completely drained. The wounded had long been taken away, but three green body bags still lay near the LZ. Almost everyone in Foit's squad was wounded in the ambush, but only a few were seriously injured.

I'd been so busy, I hadn't noticed that anyone was hurt, let alone killed. With my heart in my throat I walked over to the LZ and unzipped the first body bag. The face was unfamiliar to me. Presumably it was the driver of the lead truck. When I opened the second body bag, my stomach dropped to my knees. What little strength I had left evaporated. It was Wats, his honey-brown skin turned pale yellow. I brushed his curly hair with my hands, then closed the bag again. Sitting in the dirt, I opened the third bag. At first I thought it was Chambers, but it was Hunt, an old salt from the first platoon. With eight wounded and one dead, Foit's squad all but disappeared. Half of them would eventually return to the company.

On later occasions, Wallace's reluctance to travel the road proved to be sound judgment. A more heavily guarded convoy was attacked in almost identical fashion near the same place in the road on the same day. The lead vehicle was struck by an RPG just as it started into a curve near a hilltop, then automatic weapons opened up along the entire length of the convoy. That time the lead vehicle was a big M-48 tank. The small rocket smashed into the turret but caused little damage. The tank led the

convoy out of the kill zone while peppering the hillside
with machine-gun fire. Another tank at the rear of the
convoy blasted the hill with beehive rounds. Just around
the curve from the ambush, the convoy stopped and a
platoon of Marines came off the trucks and went after the
VC. The VC left the hill in such haste that only three
corpses were left to oppose the Marines. Given extra
motivation by the fact that it was one of our squads
among the composite platoon on the trucks, we got ready
to go out to the convoy. Though we were prepared in
only a couple of minutes, we were held at the gate. We
waited in tense and silent anticipation, wondering if we
had more friends to mourn; the trucks rolled into the base
with everyone intact. Just the same, it was a somber night
around our platoon.

The next day, another convoy was ambushed along the
same stretch of road. Again the lead vehicle was struck at
a place in the road where slow speed was required to
negotiate a curve, then the entire length of the convoy
was raked by small-arms fire. The rocket hit the gun of
the lead tank and wounded its crew, but by getting close
enough to fire an effective shot, the rocket man exposed
himself to the Marines aboard the trucks and was quickly
dispatched. Another VC, who tried to drag away the body
of his comrade, was also killed. Again the ambushers
quickly withdrew, but this time they were ambushed by
angry jets that screamed down upon them and laid a
carpet of flames across the treetops. The bomb site was
never checked, but the napalm was spread so widely it
must have cost the VC a few more lives. The proof was
that the attacks along the road were reduced to random
sniping. The VC had violated a cardinal principle of the
Vietnam War: Act predictably and you will pay. Their
predictable behavior cost many of them their lives and
left the rest of July to pass away quietly.

By the time August came around, the road was reason-
ably secure, the base was fully stocked with arms and

supplies, and our area of operation extended for many miles in all directions. Finally, four massive self-propelled 175mm cannons rumbled up the road and parked in well-prepared gun emplacements. After months of plowing a road through difficult terrain, setting up a base and fighting off the enemy, Camp Zamora was about to fulfill its mission.

But the historic first shot was not to be fired by some peon gunner. A general with two helicopters full of flunkies flew in to send a shell toward Ashau Valley. With cameras flashing, the big gun roared. "He'll probably get a Bronze Star for that," someone cynically remarked as we watched the ceremony from a distance. After a brief session of handshakes and backslapping, the nobility disappeared to the mysterious place from which they'd come.

Those of us who had been at Gio Linh did not share the jubilation with which many of the newer troops greeted the arrival of the guns. The bone-jarring concussion that followed each blast left your chest aching and ears ringing. Our regrets did not linger long. Heavy rains signaled an early start of the rainy season and turned the road into a muddy bog. The poor condition of the road threatened to strand the heavy guns at Camp Zamora and make resupply difficult. The big cannons were pulled back to Phu Bai while the road could still tolerate their weight. So there we were, out in the middle of West Hell, with all that time, money, and lives spent, and no mission.

The first two weeks of August passed without significant incident. The patrols got longer and the jungle was infested with great clouds of mosquitoes spawned by the increased rain. The first fight of the month happened on August 17. In early-morning darkness a squad from the first platoon moved from one ambush position to another. About halfway between the two positions, the point man heard human voices along the animal trail ahead of them.

The small group of Marines eased into the bush alongside the trail. Before long the voices materialized into shadowy silhouettes. When nearly on top of the Marines, the ghostly figures stopped. In a sudden flurry of shooting, two of the three VC were killed. The other one got away. The Marines were unhurt. A couple of days later a bird dog spotted a large group of VC crossing a stream made wider than normal by recent rain. Two Phantoms quickly followed and sprayed the enemy troops with rockets and cannon fire. The following day, one of our patrols found the stream littered with body parts. Arms, heads, and chunks of meat were caught among the twigs and rocks in the stream.

It had been a practice of mine, as with most Marines, to sleep with my boots on, but because August had seen so little hostile action, I decided to give my feet some air. I got off radio watch around three A.M, took off my boots, and lay down under a poncho. As soon as I got comfortable, 82mm mortars started to crash to earth all around the base. I leaped from underneath the poncho, grabbed for my boots, and dashed for a nearby foxhole. In my haste I managed to grab only one boot. After ten minutes or so the barrage ended, and the only injury was to our nerves. As I limped back to the poncho wearing only one boot, Leon insisted that it was my bare feet that caused the mortar attack. "The VC could put up with tanks, cannons, and jets, but those feet were just too much," he joked. I had sought the little bit of extra comfort not to conduct chemical warfare, as Leon had suggested, but because I felt very sick. For about a week the symptoms of an approaching cold or flu made my nights very uncomfortable. However, since I always recovered by morning, I did not complain. On a patrol the same day as the mortar attack, I attributed my feeling of fatigue and illness to a lack of sleep.

I left the camp with Wallace's squad, leading a fire team of two new guys, Bigler and Delgato. Bigler was a short, owl-eyed fellow from a well-to-do family in Milwaukee. He once wrote a letter to his father complaining of the unreliability of the Browning .45 caliber pistols that we carried, and his father sent him a brand-new Colt. Delgato was from San Antonio, a little guy who was full of energy, always working on some kind of project; he was called the "Cat" or "Cat Man." I did not look pleasantly on the patrol that was to take us deep into the jungle, miles away from the base, but was at least thankful that I didn't have to carry the radio.

We trundled through the steamy, wet jungle for hours, probing into shadowy terrain that was new to us. We followed the prescribed route as closely as possible, but there were a number of terrain features that were not on the map. When we discovered we were on a hilltop when we should have been in a valley, we knew we were lost. Even with a map and compass it was easy to get disoriented in the dark, monotonous rain forest. Thinking we were off the route by only a small degree, Wallace sought a small stream displayed on the map, to get us back on the patrol route. To be lost in Vietnam was not just an embarrassment but a life-threatening danger, the greatest of which was falling victim to friendly fire. The stream that was supposed to cut through the middle of the small valley was not there. Wallace, a by-the-book kind of guy, was reluctant to abandon the patrol, but a unified protest from the rest of the squad convinced him that we should make our way back to the road. We stumbled around the jungle until we came upon a stream we thought would lead us back to the road, but instead we only became more lost.

We knew that traveling along a stream for any distance was a dangerous thing to do, because it was a favorite place for booby traps to be placed. As we slogged down the muddy little stream in search of the road, all my strength seemed to drain away in the waist-deep water. My health faded with every torturous step. The road should have come into view a half mile down the stream, but after more than a mile of walking, it still was not in sight. My guts churning like an old washing machine, I began to shake with involuntary shivers in spite of the fact that I was drenched in sweat. When it seemed that I could not take another step, our search for the road was interrupted by the crack of an AK-47. I fell to the side of the stream, glad to stop and rest for any reason, even if it was somebody shooting at us. I was much too tired and sick to be concerned about a sniper. I just lay on my back with my rifle pointed in the general direction from which the shots had come. I looked over at Bigler and Cat Man, and they were doing the same as me. A flurry of shots rang out and a solitary VC sniper splashed into the edge of the stream. The badly wounded man was still alive when Rod pulled him to the bank, but not for long. Ivers held the sniper's head underwater until the VC was dead. "Now we don't have to carry him back," he said.

Ironically, it was the sniper who led us to the road. Apparently, the sniper had intended to practice his trade upon the passing traffic. When the first fire team left the stream to circle around to one side of the sniper, they also spotted the road. Not until we were back on it did anyone notice my condition. Wallace came over and bitched about me "skatin'," then abruptly stopped complaining and asked, "Can you make it back?" I had trouble keeping up with even the slow pace of march, but refused offers of help. Back at the base, I staggered over to the platoon CP like a drunkard returning from a night on the town, then fell to the ground when my legs would hold me up no longer.

Racked with fever and on the fringes of consciousness, I hardly noticed when Doc White removed my shirt and lifted me onto a stretcher. At the LZ, he continually poured water over me. Once on board a medevac chopper, I was immediately covered in ice from neck to ankles. The combination of ice and altitude pulled my skin tight like wet leather in the hot sun. Just the same, I arrived in Da Nang with a raging fever. I was hustled into the malaria ward of a small subterranean hospital on the edge of the airstrip. Outside, rockets crashed into the edge of the runway. Through an agonized mist I saw nurses pull a sheet over the face of the man in the bed next to me. I guess it was due to the rockets that the dead man was not removed from the room. The corpse stayed there, reminding me of my weakening hold on life. When morning came, I still alternated between shaking chills and burning fever, in a delirious world of indistinct shapes and sounds. Unable to reduce my fever, the people in Da Nang loaded me aboard a cargo plane and shipped me off to a larger facility at Cam Ranh Bay.

Sometime during days of unconsciousness, my fever finally subsided. When I finally awoke, my stomach heaved and churned and my head throbbed with pain. Madison Avenue would have been glad to hear that my deepest yearning was for some Alka-Seltzer. The first time I got out of bed to go to the head, I walked right into a wall and fell backward onto my rump. Some of the other patients laughed, but they quickly came to my assistance. I was afflicted with falciparum, one of the severest forms of malaria, and the disease had reached full maturity before I received medical attention. Consequently, there was little that could be done except to let it run its course. Paradoxically, I was one of the few people who always took the Frisbee-size pills that were supposed to help prevent contracting malaria. I took them because they were always passed out on Sunday; it helped me keep track of time.

Chapter 11

By the time I reached Cam Ranh Bay, the most dangerous part of the disease had passed. My stay at the hospital was to guard against a relapse and facilitate quick recovery of my strength. I tested my legs like a newborn deer walking out for the first time, then ventured out on a sight-seeing tour of the base. I was amazed to the point of shock at the luxurious splendor of Cam Ranh Bay. Gauged against the primitive degradation of the fire support bases where I had been, it was an Emerald City, complete with all the amenities of a modern American metropolis. In fact, there were a lot of small communities in America that did not have as fine theaters and restaurants as the base had.

However, from places where clean socks were treated like Russian sable, this transplanted Las Vegas seemed artificial and obscene. Bulging, multistory warehouses were stocked with more goodies than Sears Roebuck, and a trip to the PX was like walking through Bloomingdale's.

But above all, the most noticeable luxury of Cam Ranh Bay was the great abundance of manpower. Back in the field units, the chronic shortage of manpower influenced performance like no other factor. Here, great gangs of men strolled to libraries, went to bowling alleys, and generally lived a life quite remote from the war. Radios blared the latest tunes played over the base's own radio station. One card game had almost as many men as my platoon. While walking around, I could only think of my friends back in the jungle, living like animals while the guys here complained about the quality of the shrimp. Oddly, I hated the place and was glad to get an early release to rejoin my unit.

While waiting for a plane in Da Nang, I met yet another high school classmate. Harold Gaither had been a neighborhood rowdy with no particular plan for his future when I knew him back in Houston, but when I met him in Da Nang, he had transformed into a fine, level-headed young man. In spite of the fact that my plane was due to leave early in the morning, we talked long into the night. Between us, we were able to account for five people from our old school who were in Vietnam. I was very surprised to hear Gaither say he was considering the military as a career. I was further surprised when a fellow in the hootch lit up a joint and offered us a hit. Gaither gave him a brief lecture on the evils of drugs and told him to take it outside.

After an enjoyable night of conversation with my friend, I hopped a cargo plane to Dong Ha, then boarded southbound trucks headed for Camp Evans. Rolling past familiar sights along Highway 1, I spotted familiar faces in a sandy marsh just south of the city of Quang Tri. Hastily, I stopped the truck and reunited with my friends along the roadside; even though they were in the middle of a patrol, many of my fellow platoon members came over to welcome me back to the unit. Many old faces had left during my ten-day absence, all but Rodriguez safely. He got very sick with a severe form of dysentery and was sent to a hospital in Japan.

During his last week in the field, Sergeant Drumm had become a nervous recluse, then suddenly changed back to his old, boisterous self. Whether myth or not, it was generally believed that the first and last days in Vietnam were the most dangerous. As I dazzled the huddled group with fantastic stories of lobster dinners and the good life in Cam Ranh Bay, a short burst of automatic gunfire kicked sand at our feet. The men quickly scattered and threw a few shots into the brush across the road. No return fire came at us, and soon we were on the march as if nothing had happened. We walked for many miles until we reached the Nam Hoa Bridge, then rode shotgun for a convoy headed in the direction from which we'd just come.

Near the place I first found the platoon, we set up a defensive perimeter at a sandy graveyard on the southern bank of the Thach Han River. Almost as soon as we were in position, outraged people from a large nearby village came to us with demands that we leave the graveyard. Then, with a great deal of dignity in their strides, and holding umbrellas as insignias of authority, village leaders came out to try to succeed where the other villagers had failed. Our new platoon sergeant, Sergeant Burcher, chased them away as if they were stray chickens. With typical Vietnamese persistence, they came back repeatedly until they got an audience with our company commander. Haggling as if in the marketplace or in contract negotiations, the village leaders failed in their attempt to get us out of the graveyard, but they did secure permission to remove the bodies of their dead relatives. The news that they would do so also told us that we'd be in the area a long time.

The next day it seemed that the entire village had come to dig in the cemetery. They dug into the mounded graves like palaentologists digging for ancient fossils, and delicately placed every bone in small white boxes. Not since our stay at the Phong Dien Bridge had we been in such close contact with a large number of Vietnamese people. It was interesting, in spite of the fear and apprehension that separated us. Our discourse with the people was greatly facilitated by the assignment of Trung, an ARVN interpreter, to our platoon. Along with Leon, who had spent six weeks in language school, our linguistic capabilities were quite good. Sergeant Pascucci, our new company sergeant who took the place of Sergeant Onegin, called our interpreter "our new pet monkey." Not many adults could or would speak English, but most of the children could manage a few words, and Trung and Leon also taught many in the platoon the most useful Vietnamese words and phrases. Trung was anything but a soldier. He was much more comfortable with a guitar in his hand than a rifle. I watched him flirt with the ladies from the village and barter with vendors, and I imagined how he would fit into life back in the States. He seemed more a part of L.A. than Quang Tri.

One of our many duties during the first days of our stay at the graveyard was to inspect boat traffic along the wide, swift river that flowed nearby. Any boat that failed to land when hailed was to be sunk. A couple of hundred yards upstream from an emplacement of rocket launchers and machine guns, three Marines would call boats to the bank of the dark river. Soon, it was discovered that the coffee-colored currents offered delightful recreational possibilities, and afterward almost everyone in the platoon went for at least one ride in the fast-flowing water. We would jump into the water at the hail point and let the current carry us down to the gun position. Trung would sit along the bank and strum his guitar, but never get into the water. Citing the health hazard, Captain Rose put an end to our raucous aquatic play. We were disappointed, but fully understood the merits of the order.

After it was clear that our move into the graveyard would not be seriously challenged by the enemy, Sea-Bees arrived to start an extensive construction project. True to their names, the SeaBees swarmed over the graveyard with equipment and started in a frenzy of work almost before they got off the trucks that brought them. They were great to be around; they admired our combat role, and we admired their engineering skills. In less than a day they had plowed the sandy graveyard as flat as the Kansas plains. Their work pushed our patrols farther into the bush west of Highway 1, taking us through sparsely populated brush-covered hills that were dotted with small villages.

On our platoon's first venture into this territory, people of a small village scurried into their homes and hiding places ahead of our approach. Their quick disappearance alarmed us. The first squad deployed in a semicircle along the eastern edge of the village while the rest of the platoon moved slowly among the thatched houses. I could smell an ambush, or more accurately, I could not smell it. A cautious search revealed only huddles of cringing women and children. When a house was searched, the frightened occupants were hauled out into a central courtyard, where they quivered with greater fear each time someone was added to the group. The crowd of people clutched at each other and the children cried as Leon questioned the group about enemy presence. Thinking they might talk more freely as individuals rather than in a group, Sergeant Burcher took one young woman by the arm and pulled her toward a secluded spot between the houses. She struggled and cried hysterically.

"Stop!" Leon said. "She thinks you're going to shoot her." Suddenly, a spray of automatic gunfire came from between the houses, apparently fired to answer the woman's cries for help. The first squad returned fire while the other squad herded the villagers away from the fray. The crying woman ran right into the middle of the cross fire, toward the villagers. At great risk to himself, Sergeant Burcher chased her and tackled her to the ground, saving her from certain death.

I called in 81mm mortars to draw a curtain across the back of the ambushers' position, to make withdrawal difficult. Enemy gunfire followed us as we pushed the villagers to a nearby hilltop. With the civilians safely out of the way, I thought we would turn and counterattack. But Sergeant Burcher told me to "waste the place with artillery." I called in 105mm cannons on the interior of the village and bracketed the fringes with fire from 155mm cannons. Thunderous explosions kicked up a great cloud of dust. When the smoke cleared, the village was gone, destroyed utterly. Whether the ambushers were killed or not would never be known, but there was not a stick left standing in the village. The people were shepherded back to Highway 1, where they were sent to a sad life in a refugee camp.

I felt better about the destruction of the village, or at least I could rationalize it better, when an Alpha Company spotted three VC in the same vicinity. In classic black pajamas and military gear, the VC got away, but they led the Marines to a large cache of rice and weapons. A few days later, when another large cache of rice was discovered beneath haystacks, we concluded that the enemy intended to establish a significant presence in the area. Also in the vicinity, a squad from Alpha Company had a brief firefight with a small group of VC. In typical guerrilla fashion, the VC fired a few shots, then quickly faded into the shadows.

On the day following that little shoot-out, I was on patrol with Lane's squad in the area of the destroyed village. Because of the nature of recent enemy sightings, we'd worked out tactics to cope with small guerrilla weapons. When three quickly fired shots came at us from across a small clearing, we ran straight in the direction from which the shots had come, dividing into two columns as we went.

"I see 'em," the point man shouted before he stopped and fired fully automatic at the fleeing VC. The rapid clatter of an AK-47 sent us diving for cover. Leon fired his M-79 at a tree from behind which the bullets came, but he was so close that the round could not rotate enough to arm.

Lane realized then that only one VC had been left behind to slow us down while the others escaped. "Keep the heat on that tree," he ordered as he and Lemon crawled to one side of the solitary enemy soldier.

Two grenades exploded in quick succession and the enemy gunfire abruptly stopped. The squad rushed the tree. The VC was dead, but they shot him anyway. The new guys were so excited by the killing, they took off in pursuit of the other VC. They were completely out of control.

Lane and Ivers caught up to their squad members and brought them back, chewing them out all the way. I called for an artillery mission in the general direction in which the VC had fled, but the mission could not be fired because a bird dog had responded to our shooting and might be hit by incoming artillery shells. The little plane circled over us and then swooped low on a hill about five hundred yards ahead. The pilot spotted seven VC just before they slipped into bunkers near the crest of the hill, news of which started us moving fast in the other direction. We did not run away out of fear of the VC, but rather from the air strike that was to follow. While we were withdrawing, a camouflaged F-4 Phantom swooped on the treetops and plastered the hill with high explosives. The plane bombed and strafed the area for ten minutes, then we moved in.

Taking the long way around, we followed the tree line and prepared to assault the bunkers through a spot blown clear by a bomb. Fear was on the faces of the boys who'd been so anxious for a fight just a short time before. Smoldering and shattered, the bunkers required no assault. We reported the very effective bombing and prepared to leave when Captain Ross asked for a body count. From the near-death experience that such a request had brought when I was at Gio Linh, I was very reluctant about doing so. Pulling back some of the splintered timbers, still black and pungent with the acrid smell of spent explosives, we discovered the torn and mangled remains of an unknown number of human beings. Chopped up like tomatoes in a blender, we could not tell how many people were in the crushed bunker. Except for an arm and a head there, the hold was just a mass of ground beef. Since the bird dog had spotted seven VC, we gave the count as seven.

Almost to the hour, a week after the SeaBees arrived a big C-130 Hercules transport plane touched down on what had been the graveyard. With astonishing speed a metal airstrip and all the supporting structures were erected, transforming our little camp on the Thach Han River into a busy supply depot. Though no one told us so, we supposed that the development of the base signaled a shift from missions into the sparsely populated regions to greater efforts along the more populous coast. We were glad for the change, not so much because it was good strategy, but because the SeaBees had made the base the most livable place in which we'd ever been stationed. Albert even talked them into rigging an electric light in his bunker.

The SeaBees had all new clothing, new 782 gear, and flak jackets, which they shared most generously. In fact, they were quite fond of trading sparkling new flak jackets for grungy old ones. More important, they shared their hot food and cold drinks. Their bright and optimistic spirit was contagious, but what really drew us to them was something less obvious: they had well-defined objectives that were to be accomplished in a well-defined manner over a specific period of time, while we lived in a cloudy world of open-ended processes and amorphous strategies. We seldom even knew who commanded us above the level of the company.

The whole battalion drew together at the new base in preparation for Operation Medina, reinforcing our notion that we would concentrate on the coastal plain. Instead of working as part of one company-size unit, each platoon was spaced widely apart and we set out at breakneck speed, crashing through the brush in predawn darkness and swooping down upon villages before people went to the fields. Marching at a grueling pace with heavy packs, we surprised the first village in our path. The looks on the people's faces said so. But by the time we reached the second village, word of our approach had preceded us. We'd gone through three villages before sunup, turning each inside out, but sympathetic farmers had warned away any VC who might have been in the area.

The farther west we went, the thinner the population grew, depriving some VC of their early warning system. The flat plain turned to rolling hills as we turned south to link up with the ARVN troops in a large village. Several times, our point men reported sighting small groups of enemy soldiers. Cautiously, we approached the village where we were to link up with the ARVN company. We reached the dilapidated village right on schedule, but saw no sign of the ARVN. Except for birds and small rodents, the village was completely uninhabited. Just the same, we kept to the shadows and looked for booby traps before every step.

At the end of a dusty little road that went down the middle of the village, a large two-story structure dominated the crumbling structures all around. Even though much of the red tile roof had fallen in and the white walls were patched with green algae, it was easy to see that the building was a church. It looked too large to serve only the village, so I guessed it must have been a parish center. Just as my thoughts turned to the religious significance of the building, gunfire came from its paneless windows.

McNicoles and his squad hit the dirt and brought intense fire upon the old church. The rest of the platoon rushed forward and fired on the front and one side of the building. Two other smaller groups of enemy soldiers fired at us from the left and right, but they were all but ignored as intense attention was focused on the church. From no more than fifty yards away, Cardoluzzi fired a LAW into one of the brittle walls. As if pulled by the flaming tail of the rocket, Frost and his fire team dashed through the hole in the wall and sprayed the inside of the place with bullets. The rest of the platoon followed in a rush. We were on them so fast that all the VC were not able to get out of the back of the church before we came pouring through the doors and windows. One badly wounded VC tried gallantly to hold us back, but a blast from Rod's machine gun quickly blew his face off. Through the smoke and dust, I could hardly see the back of the church, just the spark of enemy muzzle flashes. Outside, McNicoles's squad caught VC coming out the back way. Bullets from both sides streamed through the window and sent us diving for cover. The fight faded to the monotonous rattle of one machine gun.

As it was the duty of the radio operator, I went around the platoon to check for casualties. To my surprise and pleasure, we took only one casualty during the brief but violent firefight. While making my report to the company actual, I saw a helicopter in the distant sky and had him contact the ship on the air net. The helicopter turned out to be a gunship, and arrived while I was still making the sit-rep. Wyman, with his badly injured foot, was scooped up almost before his wound was bandaged, never to be seen again.

From inside the church, five VC were dragged out front and thrown into a pile. Doc White startled Bigler with instructions to be especially careful with the man he had dragged out by the ankles. When Doc White told him that the man was still alive, Bigler dropped the man and jumped back as if the VC were a rattlesnake. The VC was covered with a lot of superficial dust, probably caused by debris from the rocket blast, and it was concussion that had injured him most. Outside the church two more VC lay dead and another was captured alive. The captive was shot up pretty badly. Both legs, his abdomen, and his back had multiple bullet wounds, but

the VC clung to life with more tenacity than he showed
in the fight.

While we waited for a medevac helicopter for the two
VC, Lane and McNicoles traded barbs, Lane contend-
ing that McNicoles was responsible for the shots that
came through the windows of the church while we were
inside. Our two captives were great prizes, because they
promised much-needed information about the location of
enemy forces in the area.

Not more than five minutes after I made the request, a
medevac helicopter arrived and hauled away the VC, the
living and the dead. In mock anger, Doc White complained that he did not have enough time to patch them
up. Except for the brief slipup when our men almost shot
each other, the assault was picture perfect. There was a
look of satisfaction on the faces of my tired platoon as we
headed out of the village.

Almost as an afterthought, Sergeant Burcher instructed
me to burn the church. I went inside and pushed bales of
straw around large wooden supports and lit them with
heat tabs that were used for cooking. Flames spread
quickly throughout the old building. Over my shoulder I
saw a pall of blue smoke spiral skyward, and my feeling
of satisfaction turned to nervous confusion. I went to
Lane, a Catholic like myself, and lamented, "I burned a
Catholic church, I burned the bones of Christ."

He was unconcerned and somewhat annoyed by my
distress. "We just killed a bunch of people back there,
Wyman got his foot shot off, and you're worried about
some rotten old building. That's some lame shit," he said.

I let loose a stream of curses. More understanding,
Abbot said that the building had not been a real church
for years. That made me feel a lot better.

The VC who fled the village ran into a platoon of
Marines who were on the way to assist us. Again they
were badly mauled. Huey gunships from the Quang Tri
airstrip made escape difficult, but the VC preferred to

face the helicopter rather than the ground troops. They ran frantically through a torrent of rockets and machine-gun fire that the helicopters poured down. The helicopters may have even helped the VC by holding back the grunts. For the small price of three dead, twenty more VC had escaped. Just the same, it must have been the blackest day ever for that particular VC unit. Another platoon of Marines that came from the Quang Tri airstrip found two badly wounded VC hidden in the bush near the place where the helicopters had killed the others. The first platoon joined us and we again tried to link up with the ARVN, but the ARVN must have known that VC were in the area; they prudently stayed away.

Once back at the base, we celebrated not only our battlefield success, but also because we were saying good-bye to some of the old salts. Hunt, Rodriguez, and Folley were toasted with contraband 101 beer and harsh Thai whiskey. They were lucky: thirteen months in some of the hottest parts of the country, and they'd made it through without serious injury. Even though they would not be safe from the war until they landed in California, they gave us hope that we, too, could survive and go home to full and productive lives. Deep into the night we sang loudly and told jokes, lampooning the salts, as was the tradition. Some of the things we joked about would have shocked people back in the States. "Could you believe how much blood that gook had? I'd plug one hole and the blood would come squirting out of another," Doc White said, sending a ripple of laughter through the bunker. In this ritual, the old salts passed on their self-confidence to those immediately behind them.

The celebration and our discussions took an unusual political turn about why we were in Vietnam. I went to Vietnam thinking of it as the Sudetenland of our time, thinking the war was the result of an imposition by an external force. After a few weeks in-country, it was abundantly clear that there would have been a war if there were no Soviet, Chinese, or even North Vietnamese intervention. The Vietnamese people were deeply divided among themselves, and it showed in our relationships with them. In some places we were received with great friendliness, and in others the hostility was so thick you could have spread it on bread. But no matter how I felt about the war, I was a U.S. Marine and would do my duty. It was the consensus of the revelers in the bunker that America should leave the Vietnamese to destroy themselves.

Chapter 12

In return for the men who left, the platoon got nine new replacements, including a new lieutenant. Lieutenant Johnson was a tall, slim young fellow with yellow-blond hair and a complexion that said he was new to Vietnam. He was only slightly older than the rest of us, in his early twenties, perhaps. He did not come on in a hard way and seemed a bit unsure of himself and his job. As a part of Operation Medina, we were still making forays deep into the countryside to the west, so he did not have time to get his feet wet or even to meet everyone in the platoon before he was thrown into command. Fortunately, he had the good sense to delegate most of the command functions to the platoon sergeant and the squad leaders while he acted as something of a technical adviser and liaison between the platoon and the company commander. I did not like Sergeant Burcher, but I thought he'd done a good job in the absence of a permanent platoon commander.

On October 9 a squad from Delta Company was hit by sniper fire as it returned from one of the long patrols to the west. A large-caliber bullet smashed into the side of a Marine's head and killed him instantly. Since we were in the area, we rushed to the scene to help the Delta platoon search the village from which the shot had come. When we arrived, the other platoon had already moved into the village and was shooting into the houses. Had their lust for revenge gone unchecked, everyone in the village would have been killed, but Lieutenant Johnson quickly

139

took control and convinced the Delta platoon to pull back while we searched the village. The way he put it was that they could act as a blocking force while we drove the VC out of the village, which offered them the possibility of satisfying their appetite for revenge. We passed through the village without finding the sniper, but by that time the high emotions had subsided enough to avert a massacre. However, two days later, I thought that Lieutenant Johnson's clever manipulation was a mistake, that everyone in the village should have been killed.

While patrolling in the same area, three shots from a sniper's rifle rang out. Two of our men fell to the ground in agony. Bigler took a bullet in the hip and Lin, a new guy, was shot in the side. Without knowing from where the shots had come, we sprayed bullets all around. Lieutenant Johnson learned the smell of blood, the sound of pain, the anger of fighting, and a few other things that could never be taught in training. The village was nearby, and it was there that I tried to affix the blame for the rash of snipings, remembering how I'd wiped out the other village with artillery fire. However, Lieutenant Johnson kept his composure and concentrated on getting help for the wounded and finishing the patrol.

The next day we were back in the village in search of the sniper, again moving from house to house, looking for something that might not be there. Trung was brought along so the villagers could be questioned. Again we went through the entire village without discovering anyone who might be guilty, then Brillig went into a house that had already been searched and gave it another try. I went along with Trung when Brillig called him to question a young woman who was in the house. Slithey pushed the woman to her knees and placed the muzzle of a .45 against her temple while Brillig turned over everything in the house. Trung badgered her with rapid-fire questions, but she was not at all intimidated and spat back answers as fast as the questions were asked. Brillig worked himself into a sweat, but found nothing. When I told him that he was holding up the platoon, he insisted there was something to be found in the house. We were about to leave anyway when Brillig again told Slithey to put a gun to the woman's head. He then went straight for one of the wooden support beams in the side of the thatch wall. After three or four vigorous kicks, the beam cracked open and out fell a well-oiled bolt-action rifle. Brillig took two quick steps and kicked the woman in the stomach. As she doubled over, Slithey hit her over the head with the pistol. He pulled her up by the bloodied hair and hit her hard across the side of her face, splitting open her cheek. Then Brillig dragged her, unconscious, out into the courtyard while I grabbed the rifle.

Again the platoon went through the village, this time like a wrecking ball, breaking up and blowing up anything that prompted even the slightest suspicion. Still, we left with only one prisoner. When I asked Brillig what had so convinced him that the woman was the sniper, he said that he had "noticed how the other people moved away from her as we approached." She was bound while still unconscious, then taken back to the airstrip, where she was turned over to the national police for further questioning. If any information came from her, we did not know it.

On October 14 the Quang Tri airstrip was hit for the first time by incoming enemy mortars. Unaccustomed to the sound of incoming fire, few of the SeaBees and new troops took cover when four 82mm mortar shells exploded on the metal runway. Twelve people were wounded, but none seriously. One of the SeaBees even seemed happy about his wound and showed it off as if it were some grand achievement.

Far away from the explosion, a hot piece of metal cut Brecht on the side of his nose. Unlike the happy SeaBee, the wound made him very angry. He cursed and vilified all Vietnamese and swore that he'd get even. Wallace, still angry about the sniping, joined Brecht in his damnation of all things Vietnamese. Together they tried to convince some of the other guys to go with them on a secret raid into the village on the south side of the base, but since most of the guys were cool to the idea, they sought other means to vent their anger and frustration. Later that night, four M-79 rounds fell indiscriminately upon the village, almost certainly the work of Wallace and Brecht. With the rising sun, a familiar and sorrowful cry rose from the village, a mournful acknowledgment that at least one of the small grenades had claimed a victim.

Operation Medina was a success not in terms of the number of enemy dead produced, but in greatly reducing enemy presence in the area and thus affording the new airstrip increased security.

During the lull after the operation, I was again shifted back to Lane's squad as a team leader to help season two of the new guys. My team was a pretty good one. Both were tough street kids from New York who took easily to the grunt's life. Both talked constantly about their lives back in New York; they shared little else. Beanardo, his name immediately contracted to Bean, told an interesting story of how he happened to be in the Marine Corps. A girlfriend by whom he had a son became angry because he started going out with another girl, and she filed an accusation of rape against him. On the strength of the false testimony from the girl's sister, Bean faced a very long time in prison for a crime which he said he did not commit. Still, he was reluctant when the judge offered him the option of joining the U.S. Marine Corps. Bean tried to bargain for the Navy, but the judge, an old jarhead, would hear none of it. We told him that he would have been better off had he gone to prison.

We ended our stay at the very comfortable new base on October 22, and reluctantly boarded trucks for the return trip to the dreaded Camp Evans. Sights along

Highway 1 were old, dull, and familiar. For some reason, we were taken off the trucks at Nam Hoa bridge and walked the rest of the way to Camp Evans. As we moved in two columns that flanked the sides of the road, we grumbled about the loss of our good living conditions at the Quang Tri airstrip and decried the relative slum that awaited us a few miles south.

The usual afternoon shower turned the road into a gummy quagmire of sticky mud. At the head of one column, Lemon noticed that water flowed around a pile of leaves on the side of the road instead of washing them away. He halted the platoon and carefully inspected the leaves. His suspicion was confirmed; it was a big booby trap, a 250-pound bomb. Anxiously, I advised Lieutenant Johnson that such booby traps were often detonated remotely by an enemy hidden nearby. Taking heed, he quickly moved the platoon back a safe distance and sent a squad to search the brush on both sides of the road. When they came back without finding anyone, he sent Wallace forward to destroy the bomb. Wallace rigged a big lump of C-4 (plastic explosive) and more than enough det cord for him to get far away from the explosion of the bomb. He lit the det cord but started back down the road at a casual walk, even stopping to light a damp cigarette. He was about halfway back when the bomb went off, sending him face first into the muddy road. Once we discovered that only his pride was injured, we laughed long and loud. For days afterward we made fun of his skills as a demolition expert.

Back at Camp Evans, we found the base in much better condition than on the occasion of our first visit, but nowhere close to the clean and orderly arrangement of the Quang Tri airstrip. We went to work right away, sending squads on long patrols in all directions. We quickly made contact with the enemy. Far to the southwest of the base, Frost's squad was taken under fire by a much larger enemy force, possibly a platoon. Our platoon headed in their direction in a hurry, balancing the danger of running into an ambush with the need for a rapid response.

"Listen to this shit; Frost is attacking!" Abbot said in astonishment after intercepting a message from Frost to the lieutenant. Undaunted by the large enemy force, Frost and his men pushed forward at what they perceived as a weak point in their line of fire. The VC immediately broke contact and withdrew into the bush, covering their path with a well-placed machine gun to make sure that the impetuous Marines did not follow.

For safety's sake, we stopped and waited for Frost and his men to link up with us instead of seeking him out at an imprecise location. The danger of someone getting shot by friendly fire was especially acute when emotions were running high. "Here comes the light-in-the-ass brigade," someone said when Frost's squad was spotted.

Amid the jokes and chuckles, Frost was warned to exercise more caution. "The NVA woulda chewed you to pieces if we were up north," Lane counseled his fellow squad leader.

Frost just gave him a gold-speckled smile and said, "I saw a chance to bring some smoke and I took it."

A new member of the squad, Micken, the only casualty of the brief fight, learned the value of caution from the encounter. A trickle of blood rolled down the side of his neck where a bullet had sliced off the bottom of one earlobe. Mick's somber silence showed that more than his ear was injured, but instead of offering understanding of his narrow escape, most of the men just joked about him getting his ear pierced. Only Doc White had the good sense to coax him to talk. From that day forward, we could always tell when Mick was not in a good mood because he would finger his notched ear. His philosophical introspection and antiwar diatribes sometimes reminded me of the Gypsy, but Mick really meant it.

The platoon got a dose of good spirits and added manpower with the return of some of the men who'd been away for treatment of wounds and illnesses. Of those to come back, Corporal Johnson had been away the longest. Wounded in fighting north of Gio Linh, he recovered from gunshot wounds to both legs and returned to us a short-timer. He told marvelous stories of the bathhouses he'd visited during his convalescence in Japan. It was from him that we first heard of the Johnson superstition.

The way he told it, anyone in our platoon named Johnson would not leave Vietnam without getting hit. Even other platoons believed that of us. I pointed out that Clarence Johnson had gone home without a scratch, and that with such a common name, there were a lot more chances for a casualty to be named Johnson.

My good friend McLean also returned to the platoon. After recovering from the grenade wound that put him in the hospital for more than a month, he was given a soft job in Battalion supply, where he could have stayed until his rotation back to the States. However, when he saw other rehabilitated Marines passing through Battalion headquarters on their way to the bush, he volunteered to go on an operation out of pangs of conscience.

Whatever the reason for his return, I was delighted to see him. He tried to play the whole thing lightly, saying that he "needed to get back into the field for a while because he was tired of the taste of Black Label beer." McLean took a lot of kidding about being a pogue, but it was clear that he was still the darling of the platoon, the guy everybody liked. The tragedy that was a few days ahead of us would erase all his feelings of guilt about working in a rear-echelon job, and send him back to Battalion supply. We had great fun renewing our friendship, then marched off to a bloodbath on Operation Granite.

The character of the whole company changed after Operation Granite, especially in our platoon. We lost so many men that the paltry few who were in fighting shape were divided between the other two platoons until ours could be brought up to strength. After the operation, Mick made a big deal of the fact that I stayed with the company when I could have been evacuated with the other wounded. I explained to him that my wounds seemed so petty when there were so many others near death. Doc White explained that he put the evac tag on my shirt because he thought the cuts on my face were signs of internal head injury. Mick always looked up to me after that.

With a batch of new replacements not long out of boot camp, and a few old hands drawn from other companies, our platoon was again back in business. The company also got a new commander, a young captain in his first combat assignment. An energetic and intelligent graduate of the Naval Academy, Captain Babel worked overtime to get the company back in top fighting condition. He did everything, from planning LPs to teaching the latest techniques of camouflage. Because Lieutenant Johnson was dead and Sergeant Burcher wounded, he even acted as our platoon commander when it was our platoon's turn to go on patrol. The one thing he did not do was ask questions.

Chapter 13

In mid-November the platoon swept through the Co Bi Than valley with the new captain directing every move and making every decision. He had a harsh and abrasive manner of command that made us long for the return of Lieutenant Burke. Marching through the waterlogged flatlands in a driving rain, we covered much of the same ground that we did at the start of Operation Granite. The second day into the patrol we discovered a large cache of food in a tunnel that had been uncovered by the heavy rain. So much food in one place could mean only that a lot of people would come along to save it from the rising water. Lane suggested that we leave the food in place and set up an ambush for whoever might come to get it. In a brief debate that followed, Captain Babel said that "it might be a month before the VC came for the food," but the rest of us knew that they would not let such a valuable commodity go to waste. At times the hungry VC in the hills had taken food from the packs of our dead friends and left guns and ammunition. Lane did not persist, he simply followed orders that we were to destroy the food as best we could.

Late in the day, we came to a stream swollen with rainwater and runoff from the mountains. After we struggled across the narrow but fast stream, I warned Captain Babel to turn back. If the stream was so difficult to negotiate, the river that lay ahead was sure to be impassable. The captain simply asked my rank and told me to get back in formation. Wallace tried to convince him of the same thing, but the captain said we could cross an old bridge upriver if the water was too high. All the old salts knew that it was very unreliable to count on a bridge that was not in our hands, yet the arrogance of our commander would not allow him to accept advice from an enlisted man. But we were Marines, we had to obey even though we knew he was wrong, even if it meant unnecessarily walking into danger.

Predictably, we soon came upon a wide expanse of water that pitched and heaved like the rapids of the Colorado River. Marching in a cold, driving rain, we took a detour toward the bridge on which Captain Babel counted to get us across the river. Although he was a toad, his dogged determination to complete the mission was admirable. Along the way, many of the troops grumbled, speculating about the condition of a bridge that we hadn't seen in months. The captain was more concerned about appearances than with the problem we faced. First, he wanted to make it clear to everyone that he was in charge; second, he did not want his first platoon patrol to return to the base without having completed its mission.

When we reached the bridge, it was in good condition but we could not get to it; the river had jumped its banks and made the bridge an island. We were forced to turn back. But we found that we could not follow the same path because the river had spilled a flood of muddy water out onto the valley. With gray daylight waning, the water rose dangerously around our knees, increasing in swiftness and depth with our every step. The situation became very perilous very quickly. Without orders, Frost took his squad in the direction of the firefight of a few days earlier. The rest of the platoon followed automatically by inertia.

Soon we were again in the foothills of the mountains of Operation Granite, safe from the flood that swirled below, but cut off from the way back to the base. Abbot started a sit-rep back to the company CP, but the captain angrily stopped him with a reminder that "I am running this platoon now."

"Well, run it!" Lane said, barely keeping his Irish temper under control.

"Maybe them VC who that food was for is right up there in them mountains," Lemon suggested.

The captain seemed paralyzed. The man with all the answers searched his map for a solution to our dilemma. While he lost himself in the map, I went to Abbot and suggested that he fake a message from the company CP that asked if we needed helicopters to take us off the hill. He played it well, first sending the request for help, then causing interruptions in the radio traffic as if there was trouble with the radio. When the captain took the handset, he had no choice but to give the coordinates to where the helicopters were to be sent. However, the heavy rain and low ceiling had grounded everything, so we would just have to stick it out on the hill until the first break in the weather.

We marched to the top of the hill and started to dig in, chopping noisily at the rain-soaked gravel. The holes filled with water faster than we could dig them. The noise apparently attracted the attention of the local sniper, who cranked off a few rounds from some unseen place. The bullets flew high overhead. We climbed into the watery holes in response, but otherwise paid him little attention. However, Captain Babel went completely insane, running and crawling all over the hill trying to prepare us for an attack. Many of the new troops were shocked and bewildered by the captain's antics, but most others ignored him the same way they did the sniper. "Maybe he sees something that we don't; after all, he is a captain," said a perplexed young rifleman who had recently joined the platoon. Micken took the occasion to get some much-needed sleep. On Lane's advice, Lemon thumped a few

M-79 rounds into the hills to quiet the faraway sniper, and so it did.

When the rain slackened, the captain had a real job to do. He had to arrange for the helicopters to pick us up. Only two old HU-34s were available to help us, so they could not take us all the way back to the base, only ferry us beyond the floodwaters. It would take three trips to carry us all to the other side of the growing flood. This maneuver called for planning and coordination and gave the captain something that settled his state of near panic. Quickly and skillfully he arranged for order and the place where each group of five men would meet the helicopters so as to maintain as much group integrity as possible.

It was dark when the first old bird landed on the top of the hill. In a procedure practiced many times during training, the first group of men was aboard the helicopters in less than three seconds.

Lane, Clark, Gomez, and I were to be the last to go across. After a half hour of waiting, we got very worried that something had gone wrong and the helicopter would not come. I had a hand flare and considered using it to signal those across the river that we were still on the hill, but recalled what had happened many months earlier, when Ivers used his cigarette lighter to signal our position. We had no radio, so there was no way of knowing what had happened. Sitting close in the darkness, we discussed whether or not we should hide in the bush until daylight or wait for the helicopter to return to the hilltop. We knew we had to come to some decision soon, because the sniper was certain to come down from the mountains to search our position for any useful items the platoon had left behind. If we killed him, we would surely alert his friends to our presence, but if we didn't, he might do it to us.

I suggested that we forget both the hill and the helicopter and try to make it back to the base on our own. We could go back into the mountains and travel west until we found a way around the floodwater. That would mean many miles of walking through territory heavily infested with enemy troops. Clark and Gomez were for my plan, but Lane, the ranking member of our group, decided we should wait on the hill a bit longer before we chose some alternative plan.

No place on earth was as lonesome as that soggy little windswept hill. We sat quietly in the drizzle, silently praying that someone on the other side of the river would realize that we were still there. We had just about decided to follow my suggestion when the churning *thump* of a helicopter blade punctuated the night. When the sound grew near, I ran to a bare spot on the hill and ignited the flare. The others were behind me in single file. A growling old HU-34 circled around the light and came in on the leeward, its belly raised against the wind. When the wheels were just about down, a series of rapidly fired shots struck at the old bird. We turned and fired in the direction we thought the shots came from. I was so angry and frustrated that I dumped a whole clip into a nearby hill.

When the shooting stopped, I could hear the helicopter circling high overhead, apparently waiting for the right moment to come in for another try. "If he doesn't come in, shoot him down," Lane yelled in anger while searching the sky with the muzzle of his rifle. A few minutes after the flare burned out, the pilot came in guided only by his memory. We sprang into the doorway almost simultaneously. The door gunner sprayed the ground with an M-60 as we lifted away. Unable to talk because of the noise, we seethed in anger at having been left on the hill for such a long time.

Instead of landing across the river where the rest of the platoon had gone, the helicopter went all the way back to Camp Evans. Our anger was swept away when we learned that the helicopter had made it back on a shoestring. The heavy loads and bad weather had strained the

ancient bird critically, and only through the resourceful-
ness of the crew was the rickety old craft able to come
and get us off the hill. Some quick field repair with
improvised parts was the only thing that got the helicopter aloft after a breakdown on the other side of the
river. I was so relieved to get back to the base that I did
not care what caused the delay. Lane was so concerned
about the rest of his squad that he didn't sleep all night,
awaiting their return. Perhaps he felt guilty about being
in relative safety while they were still at great risk. Late
the following day, the rest of the platoon dragged in,
tired, wet, and hungry, but everyone was in one piece.

We continued to run patrols through the heavily mined
valley, exercising some of the skills passed on to us by
Rogers and Sergeant Drumm to avoid booby traps. On
our first platoon-size patrol since our escape from the
flood, we found another 250-pound bomb buried alongside a trail very close to the base. On the south side of the
base Charlie Company was not so lucky: a large booby
trap exploded and killed the point man of a platoon
patrol. At least he did not suffer; he was blown to pieces
in an instant. Almost every time a squad from our platoon
went out, we found some kind of booby trap. We talked
with guys from other units to see if we were doing something different from them, in hopes that we'd discover
some special technique for finding booby traps. However, there was no magical solution. Apparently our
inherited sensitivity to the problem made our observa-
tions a bit more perceptive.

I did not know where we were going when we finally
packed up and marched out of Camp Evans, and I did not
care; I was just glad to leave. At Phu Bai, Division Headquarters, the company boarded a fleet of helicopters and
flew back to Dong Ha. Once back in my beloved Quang
Tri Province, we joined up with Alpha and Charlie companies in a march northward toward the DMZ. Booby
traps, jungles, and guerrillas were left far behind.

It was November 20 when we approached the village of Cam Lo. Our platoon was out front as we moved across a wide-open expanse of rice paddies to the east of the village. Leon crouched low and moved around the first house, then noticed that the village looked all but empty, a sure sign that trouble was afoot. Captain Babel came forward and asked Sergeant Pascucci, our new platoon sergeant, the reason for the delay. When the dangers of the situation were explained to him, the captain surprised us by making a good decision. The village showed signs of enemy presence, so we would approach from the north through an area that offered more cover and concealment. However, Abbot winced at the message that came back from battalion headquarters. For once our shithead company commander had made a good decision, and it was negated by even bigger shitheads. We were to enter the village from the east. We cursed the poor judgment and blamed it on laziness of top commanders to rework plans to fit the situation. But we were Marines, so we obeyed.

Certain that enemy troops lurked somewhere ahead, we spread the wedge formation as widely as possible and Sergeant Pascucci guided our platoon as far away from the village as he could. We scanned the bush with wide apprehensive eyes and spoke in whispers, even though everyone in the province knew we were there. Sure enough, when the main body of the formation came close to the edge of the village, enemy rifles and machine guns opened up. Those closest to the village were already on the ground.

Lying flat in the short grass between the rice paddies, I judged the enemy to be very weak and called my team up so we could return fire in concert. The rest of the squad followed them and fell into a long line that perforated the little huts on the edge of the village. The rest of the platoon inched forward behind them, trying to move closer and keep the enemy pinned down at the same time. From far behind, I heard Captain Babel scream something that I couldn't understand. I could not see the enemy at all, so I just fired in the general direction I thought would be effective. Lane directed everyone to cover the field of fire in front of them. "They're running!" Gomez shouted as he came to one knee and fired furiously at a target I could not see. I yelled for him to get back down, and he quickly obeyed.

As soon as the enemy shooting stopped, we heard the familiar swish of incoming mortars. The rapidly fired M-60 mortars sent us scurrying backward a lot faster than we'd moved forward. About ten widely dispersed rounds exploded without harming anyone, but effectively covered the withdrawal of whoever had fired at us. When the barrage lifted, the unseen enemy was gone. We lifted ourselves from the grass and checked each other to make sure everyone was all right. The shooting had left eleven men wounded, but only two were injured seriously enough to leave the company. Needless to say, everyone was angry to the point of boiling when we moved through the village, and would have vented that anger on the people who lived there had we not had to keep moving. The farther north we marched, the fewer signs of civilian habitation were apparent. The fields of grass and rice paddies turned to a rolling entanglement of thorny bushes and small trees and forced our unwieldy wedge formation into a ragged column.

Under the blazing heat of a midday sun, a wild flurry of gunfire erupted from the brush about fifty yards ahead of the point man in our platoon. Again we poured back fire at an unseen enemy who quickly faded away. At the front of the formation, Brewster and Micken lay sprawled in the weeds, both shot in the chest. Mick lay motionless as Doc White slapped a piece of aluminum foil over the spurting wound; only his eyes betrayed his intense struggle to stay alive. Nearby, Brewster protested Doc McDonald's attention and even tried to get to his feet. Far at the rear of the formation, the sergeant for the first platoon had taken a couple of bullets in the mid-section. Medevac helicopters arrived very quickly from nearby Dong Ha, raising our hopes for our badly injured friends, but it was too late for Brewster. He died while being put aboard the helicopter. The platoon sergeant died on the operating table in Dong Ha. It was later rumored that someone in the first platoon had settled an old vendetta with the sergeant, taking advantage of the hostile situation to murder him.

Chapter 14

In a slow, steady rain that gradually washed the heat from our bodies, we again returned to the firebreak that had been cut for the ill-fated McNamara Line. Out in the bush between Con Thien and Gio Linh, all the companies in the battalion slowly drifted together, bringing an end to Operation Kentucky, as our march was called. On one meal a day, it was a hungry and uncomfortable time when we got the opportunity to renew old friendships with guys in other units.

My friend from home, Alfred Major, was as bright and cheerful as ever, in spite of the hardships. He told me of yet another of our classmates he had seen in Cam Lo, a fellow by the name of Irving Smith. He met Irving on the road to Dong Ha, where the latter was to get treatment for damage to his eyes from having a flare ignite close to his face. Irv would never return to his unit, 2/26, because his eye damage resulted in very poor night vision. Years later I met him again in Houston. He was nearly blind.

Chambers had not changed a bit, still loquacious, still jocular, and still skinny as a rail. With an endless stream of jokes, he forced everyone to celebrate his last few days in the field. He even turned our stomach rumblings into a source of humor, yet that was not enough to wipe away the hunger that went along with dim-rats (diminished rations). What's more, the constant rain of the winter monsoon made me shiver with cold, and the wetness made my fingers crack open around the fingernails.

Spread out over more than a mile, the battalion drifted back and forth along the southern edge of the DMZ in some grand design unknown to the common troops. A few miles from Con Thien we turned north and linked up with 2/9 at a place close to the border. Two battalions in one place was the largest force I'd ever seen. There were so many people roaming through the hills that I expected artillery to come our way, but I guess we kept moving too much for the enemy gunners to get a good fix on us. Just the same, I kept my ears tuned for the sound of enemy cannons.

As far as we could figure, the strategy of our leaders was to place enough people in precarious positions to induce the enemy to attack. Again, the reliance on firepower as a substitute for creative thinking was the usual arrangement. The NVA had to have the most advantageous terrain, preplotted artillery targets, all the manpower they needed, and a well-rehearsed plan of attack. We got to march up and down until someone shot at us.

On December 6 lead elements of Delta Company spotted a small group of NVA just as they dashed from a clearing into a covering of bushes. Word of the sighting pulsed through the ranks like an electrical charge. We feared that this was not just an accidental encounter, but the prelude to something much bigger. "They must be trying to draw us close" was the word that circulated through the ranks.

Delta Company sent a platoon to search out the NVA, while the rest of the battalion closed in on the area. The fast-pursuing Marines got close enough to the enemy troops to see the last of them disappear into a row of camouflaged bunkers. When the Marines stopped to wait for the arrival of help, the NVA opened up with 60mm mortars and machine guns. The rest of Delta Company quickly arrived and peppered the bunkers with gunfire, then they pulled back and struck at the bunkers with artillery fire. When the dust cleared, the Marines swept through the area, firing LAWs at the bunkers that survived the bombardment; but only a few enemy troops remained by the time the Marines returned. Inside one bunker, bullets shattered a radio and sent up a shower of sparks. The assault was quickly concluded, because the NVA withdrew during the artillery barrage. From inside the bunkers ten dead NVA troops were pulled; three others were killed in the tall grass behind. For that victory, Delta Company paid the price of one dead and one wounded.

For the next few days we marched back and forth along the DMZ, stopping at various points to set up defensive positions. Our rations went from one box of C-rations a day to half a box a day, because the bad weather made resupply very difficult. Then the rations were reduced to a half box every other day, adding yet another layer of misery to the cold, fatigue, and wetness that accompanied us along the operation.

Lane, Abbot, and I did the worst thing possible, we talked about food. Our conversations were dominated by detailed descriptions of our favorite meals. My soggy feet reminded me of the days when, as a small boy, I spent hours wading through marshes and ditches to catch crayfish, which my mother would transform into the most delectable bisque or étouffée. Our conversations also reminded me of Cardoluzzi. He and I had frequently discussed our mothers' culinary habits, which sounded surprisingly similar. Like my mother, his was a shy young woman married to a much older and outgoing man. I lost my mother at a very young age, and now this woman in New York had lost her son.

Though the temperature was probably no colder than sixty-five degrees, constant exposure to the elements over a long period of time made the night air seem as cold as a Minnesota winter. Even Abbot, who was accustomed to the cold winters of Old Lyme, Connecticut, shivered in the frigid, wet nights. One night when the rain was particularly heavy, Thorston started to whine and complain as if the circumstances were miserable for him alone. I nudged Lane in anticipation as Frost walked slowly toward his whimpering squad member, but instead of slugging Thorston, Frost took off his poncho and draped it over Thorston's shoulders, consoling him with kind words of better times to come. Lemon was flabbergasted that Thorston would accept Frost's poncho and called him a "candyass fab." I hated Thorston; he was a goldbricking skate who always courted favors from others around him, and he was undependable in a fight. He was the worst of the new guys to come to the platoon, many of whom got very sick on the operation but quietly endured their misery. Unaccustomed to the privations and hardships of field life, a great many of them were stricken with dysentery, yet most of them performed their duties well.

When the battalion started to break up into companies and head off in different directions, I hoped that we would head for one of the nearby bases so the sick guys could have a chance to recover. However, our company just walked in a big circle and came back to the same place we'd camped the previous night. Early the next morning the cloudy sky finally opened up and let a few rays of sunshine through. Before we could celebrate the return of the long-absent sun, the long-silent guns across the border hurled a barrage of shells that crashed to the earth near the southern edge of our defensive perimeter. The soggy earth quivered like Jell-O and sucked up most of the shrapnel from the explosions while we crouched low in shallow holes. More accurately aimed 82mm mortars fell within our midst, forcing some to move out of the shallow holes and seek better cover in a nearby stand of trees. My God! I wish I had dug this hole a little deeper, I thought.

When Frost took cover behind a large fallen tree, he was shocked by the sight of an NVA platoon coming straight at him. He and the rest of his squad opened up on the enemy with less than a hundred yards between them. I rushed over and saw them approaching on a broad front all along the north side of the perimeter. Hundreds of them fired at us from the trees and bushes. Anticipating a long fight, Lane shouted for us to conserve our ammo.

Then suddenly they were there in front of us, not even camouflaged, just pith helmets and rifles. My heart pounded furiously, yet I was able to overcome my anxiety and fire at the darting figures in a very controlled way. Up and down the line everybody was yelling and shouting, some trying to find out if we would defend or attack, and others just to lift their spirits. Gunfire chattered wildly all around and bullets zipped continuously past my ears. Some squads started to move forward, while others retreated before intense enemy fire that was intended to punch holes in the line at specific points. Incoming 82mm mortars again swished and exploded all around our position. The situation was even more chaotic than most battles.

Lane yelled at Abbot to get some artillery on the position in front of us, but all the platoons had called for artillery mission. The situation on the radio was just as confused as that on the field. Chips of wood flew off the fallen tree and kicked up dirt all around us as the NVA drew more troops to close quarters. "Get the captain up here!" Lane yelled to me. Staying as low as I could, I scurried to our company commander's position and was shocked to find that he was lying on his back in the bottom of a foxhole. There we were, under attack by at least a battalion of enemy troops, and our leader was trying to become a gopher. I was astonished and disgusted at the same time.

When I told him that he was needed at our platoon, the captain yelled up at me, "Get down, you damn fool. That's an order."

My composure instantly evaporated in a flash of anger

and I raised my rifle butt to hit Captain Babel, but took hold of myself and snapped back, "How can you give me orders from down in a hole?" I then stood up as straight as I could and walked back to our platoon with bullets zipping past.

Lane repeated the captain's order. As soon as I got down, an enemy rocket cut the tree in half and knocked several men backward, but they just got up and kept firing back.

"Grenade!" Douglas shouted, and we ducked behind the log, then sprang back up after the explosion and sprayed full-out. Beside me, Lemon's eyes grew to the size of billiard balls because he knew that if the enemy was close enough to throw grenades, they were right on top of us. Gomez wore a crazed smile. I dumped a full clip and changed magazines almost before the last bullet could pass through the barrel. About fifty yards ahead of me, I saw NVA troops lying in the grass and bushes. There was another series of explosions behind me, from mortars or grenades, but all my attention was focused on the men in front of me. Sergeant Pascucci had arranged the platoon in a relatively unified front, which put up a wall of bullets against the approaching enemy. Then, in concert, the enemy soldiers suddenly broke off to the right, all along the line. A single NVA soldier lay dead about ten feet in front of our position. Lane told Bean to retrieve the body, but Bean would have no part of it. Angrily, Lane pumped three more bullets into the body and repeated the order. Bean obeyed, snatching back the corpse like a leopard with its prey.

Within minutes all shooting stopped. Men with wounds of varying severity were rushed to a clearing that was to be our LZ, and within minutes an old HU-34 clattered in to pick them up. The old bird started to pull away when a rocket flashed in from a nearby tree line and cut off its tail. It fell to the ground with a heavy *thump* and jumped up again. It did this repeatedly, and wounded men and crewmen were tossed all around the LZ while the helicopter tore itself apart. The main rotor wobbled back and forth, throwing up splinters of itself each time it hit the ground.

While the helicopter was hopping up and down, the second platoon opened fire on the stand of trees and killed the enemy soldiers who were there. When the helicopter finally stopped thrashing about, it was hardly recognizable as an aircraft. It was a near miracle that none of the men on board were killed. A Huey arrived shortly afterward and took the wounded away from the renewed shooting. Throughout the day, small groups of enemy soldiers would strike at various places along the lines, then quickly pull back. Artillery fire from Con Thien and Gio Linh blasted the area all day long.

The conditions were perfect for the enemy to sneak close and mount an attack. I supposed that we hadn't been moved because the brass wanted the enemy to attack. It ran through my mind that the attack of the day was only to test our strength and check our deployment in preparation for the real attack that was to come under the cover of darkness. We had thrown out a very strong defense, but that was still not reason enough for the NVA to withhold an assault.

In the claustrophobic shroud of fog that night, no one slept. Suddenly, the night was punctuated by a muffled explosion. All the rifles came up, ready to repel the anticipated attack, but nothing happened and no shots were fired. A few seconds after the explosion, the near-hysterical voice of Thorston screamed for help over the radio. Wisely, Captain Babel told the men to hold their position and told Thorston not to fire at anything he could not see because other platoons had LPs in the area.

Moments later Thorston and Gomez came crashing noisily through the brush, dragging Bean. In a near panic, Thorston forgot or ignored the password, pulled away from Bean's limp arm, and ran for the line, leaving Gomez to carry Bean the rest of the way. Bean's face and chest were covered with blood that poured down from a wound that split the bridge of his nose all the way up to the eyebrow.

Doc White tried desperately to pinch the wound closed while at the same time sucking blood from Bean's nose and mouth. Doc spat blood on the ground and Bean started breathing again. Abbot hurriedly summoned a medevac. When it seemed that Bean would make it, he let out a long gurgling noise and died. Doc White kept working, pounding his chest, trying to get his heart started again, but it was in vain. The skinny medic's face contorted and tears cut a trail down his blood-covered skin.

Abbot canceled the medevac, and he and I carried the body of our friend to the LZ, where it would be picked up in the morning. I wanted to cry, but I just could not. I felt terrible, but couldn't push out the tears. I could only think that the judge who sent Bean to the Marine Corps had sentenced him to death. On the way back I paused to listen to Gomez's explanation of the tragedy as he told it to Sergeant Pascucci. His account was simple. As soon as they reached the position, they sat with their backs to each other and placed the radio in the middle of the small circle. Bean had the first watch, so the other two lay down to get some rest. Just as they did, a grenade went off and the footsteps of someone rushing away could be heard moving through the bush.

The tension and fear I'd felt earlier changed to apathy. As I sat indifferently awaiting the imminent attack, Lane came from a meeting with the captain with news that a TPQ (a type of high altitude radar-directed bombing) mission would strike at the area just north of us. No sooner had he disappeared in the mist than the earth quaked under a long series of loud explosions. Between the resonating eruptions of each bomb I could hear the loudly screamed distress call, "Raymond! Raymond!" A stray bomb had fallen on the second platoon and instantly obliterated eight Marines and wounded two others.

Then, the acrid smell of cordite still in the air, enemy troops opened up all around the perimeter. The firing was from such close quarters that at first I thought it was mistakenly directed from one of our own units. Beside me, Gomez took a round in the top of one shoulder and was quickly dragged away by Doc McDonald. I covered his field of fire with a steady stream of bullets until Lane came by with orders to cease fire. The first rays of morning light had started to rise above the horizon before all the shooting stopped. In the dim light of dawn, search parties from each of our platoons went through the nearby brush to look for NVA. No live NVA were found around our lines, only twenty dead ones.

Finding that the enemy had withdrawn, attention was turned to the evacuation of our dead and wounded. At the LZ, five more body bags lay beside Bean's corpse. A few miles from our company, Charlie Company suffered twenty-seven casualties in a similar attack. Fortunately for them, none were fatal. Our company suffered ten wounded, one of which was a psychological casualty. When the misplaced bomb exploded, something snapped in Thorston's mind, sending him into a world where he could not see the danger all around him. The tragedy of the LP, the greater tragedy of the bombing, and the tense waiting sent him into a catatonic stupor. Abbot held his hand and led him to the LZ.

An HU-46 landed and dumped out a load of C-rations, then started to take on the wounded, when someone shouted, "Incoming!" Mortar rounds exploded near the LZ. The helicopter unexpectedly lifted away, spilling wounded men to the ground from fifteen feet or more. Thorston broke loose from Abbot and ran erratically all over the place. I rushed over and tackled him to the ground. With his eyes tightly closed and his hands over his ears,

Thorston screamed in terror. I felt so sorry for him, and guilty that I'd resented him in the past.

By noon we finally got all the sick and wounded evacuated and were again on the march, passing close to the north side of Con Thien, seeing the base from the same perspective that many enemy soldiers had. About a mile farther west we stopped to rest in the shade of a stand of small trees. Just as we did, the lead squad from the company came under fire from a small group of NVA soldiers in a trench line to the south. Quickly, our platoon swept around to one side of the trench and returned fire on the enemy. At once we realized that this small group was alone, and we closed tightly upon them to prevent their fleeing south. With the second platoon firing from the west and us firing from the east, the NVA were in a hopeless position.

Then we got the amazing orders to cease fire and pull back. Apparently, an artillery mission was to be fired on the trench, but we knew that the NVA soldiers would not just sit around and wait for the artillery if there was no pressure on them. For once we had the numerical and tactical advantage, and we were not about to give it up; so when the second platoon stopped shouting, we rushed the trench line, firing with such intensity that the NVA could hardly raise their heads above the cover of the trench. From very close range we flooded the trench with bullets and grenades. Crawling slowly, Frost led his squad on the final approach. We thought the trench might be the entrance to a large underground bunker complex, but it turned out to be only an old irrigation ditch. Seven NVA troops lay sprawled in the ditch, all dead but one. Doc White dragged the wounded enemy from the trench and deposited him on a bare patch of ground, but instead of working on him, he just looked on in amazement. "Can you believe this guy is alive with all those holes in him?" he asked of the guys who stood nearby. The man died while we counted the number of times he'd been hit—forty-five bullets and he was still alive, at least for a few minutes.

The NVA had fired on our lead squad without knowing the whole company was in the trees, and were wiped out. In the blood-drenched trench I found a photograph, apparently of the parents of one of the dead men. The grainy picture made me feel very uneasy; it was an unwanted reminder that our enemies were people just like everyone else, so I quickly tore it up. After collecting weapons and papers, we marched away in the direction of a fire support base called C2, leaving the bodies of the enemy soldiers to rot in the ditch. I wondered if the people in the photograph would ever learn what happened to their son.

In the middle of December, we walked into C1, a fire support base about a mile directly south of Con Thien. North Vietnamese gunners welcomed us to the base with repeated salvos of their artillery, which we hadn't experienced for some time. Day after day big 130mm and 152mm shells rocked the base, sending up tall clouds of dust and smoke. With all the shelling, casualties inevitably followed. In the first light of early morning, eight big shells arrived at C2 just as men from an LP did the same. Burton, a longtime member of the first platoon, was badly injured by one of the shells that exploded on the road near the south side of the base. His chest was hacked upon by a big piece of metal, one leg was mangled to a ragged mess, and one of his eyes was destroyed.

While carrying supplies dropped from a helicopter, Windfree, one of the new guys in our platoon, was cut down by a heavy barrage of 60mm mortars. After several days of bombardment by the small mortars, our mortar men developed a good guess as to where the enemy tube was and responded with shells of their own while enemy rounds were still in the air. A patrol sent to check the suspected area found the damaged base plate of a 60mm mortar tube and three of the fingers that had apparently held it in place.

In the days that followed, our patrols frequently found the bodies of NVA troops who had ventured too close to the base and fell victim to our mortars. The regular bombardment of C2 soon developed a two-level rhythm: light artillery and mortars fell during the mornings, and big shells struck during the evenings and nights. It was Gio Linh all over again. In nearly a year of fighting, nothing had changed but the faces.

On the outside I was almost a year older, but inside I was already an old man. I stood on a hill in the middle of C2 looking south at two Hueys that rose and fell on some unknown target and wondered about the futility of the unchanging scene. When later that night, around 2200, a two-hundred-round barrage quivered the hill with successive shock waves, I did not even interrupt the letter that I was composing. It all seemed so natural to me; even when I learned that thirteen men in the company had been wounded in the barrage, it seemed like just the way things were supposed to be.

Early the next morning a single shell whistled in from the north and exploded near the south gate, where a small group of new replacements had the misfortune to be. I ran toward the familiar and desperate cry for help and found a corpsman already working on a circle of badly injured men. In the middle of the road was the body of a slender black man, cut in half by the explosion. I checked for the dog tag on the corpse and didn't find it, so I asked one of the wounded men the identity of the dead man. Remembering that Flash was to lead the new guys back to our platoon, I asked if the dead man had called himself "Flash." The wounded man answered affirmatively. I ran back to the platoon area and sent a KIA report to the company, but I wasn't sure I'd gotten Flash's real name correctly, so I went to his bunkmate, Vass. In the bunker nearest the road, I did not find Vass, who was away at a dice game in another bunker; but there, sleeping soundly on a bed of sandbags, was Flash! I snatched him out of his bunk, gave him a big hug, and ran toward the company CP to intercept the mistaken KIA report.

Flash had earned his nickname because of his slowness, and that very quality had saved his life. The poor dead soul on the road turned out to have been one of the replacements, killed before we could even learn his name. I retrieved the KIA report, took it back to the platoon, and showed it to Flash and the others, as much to show that my odd behavior was not a loose wire come unraveled as to tell what happened. Deep into the night we celebrated Flash's return from the dead with old songs, sung loudly and poorly.

Chapter 15

In the days that followed, a great weight was lifted from the company by the early departure of Captain Babel. He was technically good and had a quick mind, but he could not cut it as a field commander. His replacement, Captain Ross, was an older man who had served as an enlisted man during the Korean War, which held out great hope to us. Along with a bunch of new riflemen, our platoon got a new commander and sergeant. Sergeant Pascucci was promoted and put in charge of company supply. Our new platoon sergeant was an old guy with almost twenty years of service behind him. The new platoon commander was a big, goofy fellow fresh out of officer training school. Lieutenant Proust brought with him all kinds of silly John Wayne images; it was clear that Sergeant Wilson just wanted to put in his time and get out.

At that time, most units of the battalion were very close together, strung out along Route 9 on a north-to-south axis from Con Thien in the north to Cam Lo in the south. Alpha Company was at Con Thien, Charlie Company at A1, Bravo Company at C2, and Delta Company at the end of the line at Cam Lo. None of these bases was far from the other. Frequent travel along Route 9 facilitated contact among troopers from different units of the battalion and gave us the feeling of being a part of one group. My friend, Alfred Major, took a road escort south so he could visit me. He brought another fellow from Houston, Bryan Whitehead. Bryan was with Force Recon, and looked it. A short, powerfully built guy, he was more than suited for any physical demand that his tough job might place on him. Yet his brawn was not what made the most notable impression on me when I first met him: it was his intellectual adroitness. Instead of focusing on common things back home, we mainly talked about our literary interests, his being much loftier than mine. I gave him a copy of a Dashiel Hammett novel in return for *The Brothers Karamazov*. Bryan had decided to go to college at Texas Southern University, a few blocks from where he lived in Houston. We talked about that and how old we would seem compared with other people our age. We became good friends and made it a point to see each other whenever our duties brought us close to each other. We were a source of great comfort to each other, a reminder that all was not madness, that we could soon go home and be normal people.

The platoon was as close to full strength as I'd ever seen it, and, even better, most of the new guys were level-headed fellows. To get some field experience for the newcomers, Captain Ross sent out a lot of small patrols close to the base. On one such patrol, I carried the radio for Lane's squad as we left the base in the dark of early morning. I watched the new guys closely to see if they moved with ease and alertness. As expected, they were a bit tense; however, they did all the right things. When we stopped, no one had to tell them to get down, they made good use of shadows, and moved well in general.

Out on point, Lemon stopped suddenly and went down on one knee. Everyone behind slowly and quietly sank into the grass along with him. Lemon had caught a flicker of movement in the brush about fifty yards directly ahead of us, which he signaled simply by pointing his finger. I buried the handset of the radio into my stomach so no noise would give us away. Though we were only about five hundred yards from the base, we were very much aware that Lemon's sighting could be a small part of a very large dragon.

Lane signaled for the last fire team to move to one side so the men at the rear of the column could fire straight ahead if necessary. Douglas started to stand up, but I pulled him back to the ground. His jaw hung slack and his eyes were as big as silver dollars. Suddenly, a single NVA soldier bolted from a cluster of thick bushes and raced away from us toward another thicket. Everyone in the squad opened up. I quickly scanned the surrounding brush for enemy soldiers other than the one in front of us. Bullets thrashed at the back of the fleeing soldier, ending his life in mid-stride. We were surprised and pleased to discover that he was alone.

When Captain Ross told us to bring the body back to the base, I thought, Here we go again, more geek fascination with bodies. However, the captain wanted to see if the dead man was a regular soldier or some kind of specialist. A search of the bullet-riddled body revealed very frightening papers. From one pocket of the baggy green uniform came a very detailed sketch of C1. Our first thought was that the map meant a ground attack was soon to come, but Captain Ross told us it looked more like an artillery plan.

The captain's assessment seemed correct, because shortly afterward, two large shells scored direct hits on the company CP bunker, then three big shells struck at our section of the perimeter, shrouding the bunkers of our platoon in a cloud of dust and smoke. One of our bunkers was left a mound of rubble, with one of the two occupants badly injured. With only a week left in the field, O'Corn lost most of one arm and had one hip crushed. Colletta was hardly scratched, just a little punchy from the concussion, but with him it was hard to tell the difference.

A lot had been learned about constructing bunkers since the days back at Gio Linh, a fact that undoubtedly saved at least two lives among us. The low profiles, sloping exterior wall, and slanted interior walls of the new bunkers absorbed and dissipated much of the energy of artillery rounds. The tops of the bunker were made of sandbag layers with empty ammo boxes in between to act as shock absorbers. C2 was relatively new and stood up well to bombardment by heavy artillery, which became a daily event. Once again we lived like prairie dogs, scurrying underground when the menace of artillery was in the air. While on an idiotic detail to clean up paper, Leon was caught in the open when some of the daily bombardment started. Shrapnel from a large shell sliced open his lower abdomen and spilled his intestines from the gaping wound. The rush to the LZ was too late; he died before the helicopter arrived. My thoughts went back to the day when I unloaded dead and wounded men from helicopters in Dong Ha. Now the blood of my old friend would stain the helicopter floor and give trepidation to some newcomer.

Four days before Christmas, most of the company left C2 on a long-range patrol toward Khe Sanh, passing through an area where an Alpha Company squad had clashed with a platoon of NVA only a few days earlier. Six NVA troops had been killed at no cost to the Marines, so we thought the enemy might still be lurking about to seek some revenge. Heavily laden with the extra provisions and ammunition common to long patrols, we moved clumsily. Most people carried about four hundred rounds of ammunition, but I carried twice as much because I was afraid we'd suffer the same kinds of shortages as before we came to C1. Possibly, the extra ammo was meant to give me a sense of security I desperately needed.

I carried the radio for Lieutenant Proust near the rear of the platoon, while Abbot was up front with Sergeant Wilson. When we passed the first checkpoint, I reported as much to the captain, as was the custom and as I'd done on hundreds of patrols previously. But Lieutenant Proust got very angry and ordered me to make no transmissions without his prior approval. He gave Abbot a similar scolding. So Abbot and I had said nothing to him for most of the day, not even when the lieutenant screwed things up, like mixing up the codes. But then our new platoon commander started to make mistakes that were not just procedural, but endangered others.

After giving me my comeuppance, he headed out directly across an open rice paddy, directing the platoon before him. He felt it safe to walk in the open because the first platoon had moved through the area ahead of us. As if that was not foolish enough, he pulled out a map when we were in the middle of the rice paddy. I lingered behind and let him get as far away from me as I could. Waving a map in the face of a sniper was like waving a cape before a bull; it was a sure sign of a unit leader. We crossed the rice paddy without incident and moved into a small stand of trees that concealed a number of large holes in the ground. Lieutenant Proust walked from one hole to the other over and over again, becoming more and more perplexed as to what action should be taken each time he poked his nose into a hole. Finally, Wallace went to him and pointed out a few things to look for in such circumstances. There were no scratches or marks around the holes, he noted, the surrounding grass and bushes were not broken or trampled, and an old growth of moss and lichen went deep into the holes. The obvious conclusion he meant to point out was that the holes had not been used in a very long time. But that conclusion was ignored by the lieutenant, who continued walking back and forth like a golfer studying a difficult putt.

Pressing his foot into the soft earth around the mouth of the hole, Wallace showed the resultant print to our goofy commander to convince him that even if there were a tunnel complex underneath, no one had recently passed this way. Unimpressed, Lieutenant Proust told

Wallace to send a couple of his men down into the hole. Captain Ross arrived with the rear guard and really chewed out the lieutenant when he found out the reason for the delay. The captain had called orders for the lieutenant to mark the holes on the map and keep moving, but I deliberately withheld the message to get the lieutenant in trouble.

Later in the day, Douglas spotted an NVA soldier with leaf camouflage about a hundred yards directly in front of us. In a flash of alarm, Douglas fell to the ground and fired at the place in the bushes where he saw the enemy soldier disappear. We fell to the ground in anticipation of return fire, which did not come. Frost sent Colletta and Tisby forward. They crawled the long distance to the bushes, then signaled the rest of us forward. A leaf-covered enemy soldier lay dead from a single bullet that passed completely through his head. Lieutenant Proust was mesmerized by the dead man, unaware that control of the platoon had passed from him to the squad leader. About a mile away, Charlie Company had clashed with a small NVA unit in which rifle fire, rockets, and 60mm mortars were exchanged. Two Marines were wounded and two NVA soldiers were killed.

Out in the scrub bush country along the DMZ, a cloudy Christmas arrived almost unnoticed, just another day of humping the hills on the way back to C2. Our only Christmas gift was given to us by the North Vietnamese, a suspension of the daily bombardment that hammered at every base along the DMZ. The final days of 1967 passed quietly, like an old boxer past his prime, exhausted and drained.

For about two weeks after the new year, fighting near our base virtually ceased. During the lull in fighting, Alfred Major and I arranged for all the Houston guys in the battalion to meet at Cam Lo, a convenient place because that was where men from the northern bases could meet men from Dong Ha. I went from C2 along with a small group that rode shotgun for a convoy of trucks. When I got there, I found that the Houston meeting had become a Houston/Dallas/San Antonio meeting, a party of about twenty men in loud progress. It was great fun, especially when someone produced a tape recorder and a bag of cassettes. Everyone had something they wanted to hear, the Temptations, the Four Tops, James Brown; but it was the music of Jimi Hendrix that we felt most. Our little party lasted only a couple of hours, because most of the guys had to catch transportation back to their units before nightfall stopped all traffic on the road.

The peaceful interlude was abruptly ended on January 24, when a jeep was knocked off the road in a ball of flames. One man was killed outright by the rocket, and another was killed by the withering gunfire that followed. A third lay motionless on the scorched ground, badly injured but still alive. Two men from an Army artillery battery, who had traveled closely behind in another jeep, soon found themselves in the middle of an ambush. They stopped only long enough to scoop up the wounded man on the road, then raced the short distance to C2. Alerted by the sound of gunfire, the platoon was already prepared to move out when the bullet-pocked jeep came barreling through the south gate.

No one needed orders to tell them what to do; we knew what came next. The squads of Wallace and Frost climbed aboard a twin 40mm duster and an M-48 tank. I carried the radio. Within minutes we were at the overturned jeep, and the duster started spitting red 40mm shells along both sides of the road. The squads fanned out behind the protective fire in search of the ambusher. Finding no one to fight, we collected the dead Marines and went back to C2.

The next day two trucks were ambushed near the same place in the road where the jeep had been struck, but this time we were ready for them. Two squads were already

out on patrol in the area. The rest of our platoon rushed to
vehicles that had been placed near the south gate to
reduce our response time. With less caution than the day
before, we leaped off the trucks and hosed down the surrounding area with widely dispersed gunfire. Without
seeing anyone, we killed four NVA soldiers, then loaded
the cargo of C-rations onto our trucks. A big M-48 tank
came up the road, and when we were far enough away, it
fired a couple of 90mm shells, which tore the disabled
truck apart. In the back of the truck on which I rode,
Brecht impassively watched the pall of smoke grow skyward, his feet resting atop the Vietnamese corpses. He
bore little resemblance to the Howdy Doody–faced
farmboy that he'd been when he first joined the platoon
many months earlier.

The bold enemy attacks along the road between Cam
Lo and C2 caused some adjustments in the traffic. Large
convoys escorted by contingents of riflemen were substi-
tuted for the haphazard method. From lessons learned at
Camp Zamora, the roadside was periodically blasted
with heavy mortar fire just ahead of the passage of a
convoy. On one such convoy, I carried the radio for
Lane's squad aboard trucks headed for Dong Ha.

We left C2 in the late evening of February 2, ten men
to guard five trucks. When we reached Cam Lo, we could
go no farther because heavy cloud cover had brought
on darkness earlier than usual. That was very good news
to us, because it left us with no duties for an entire night,
a rare and most cherished luxury. Lane reported to
the Delta Company CP while the rest of us found comfortable places in a trench line near the gate. A few fellows drifted off to sleep right away while others visited
friends in Delta Company. I hadn't slept through a complete night for so long that I did not think I could do it.
Exempting ourselves from the one-man watch rotation
that was to act as a lookout for our little squad, Lane and

I went to sleep early, looking forward to getting a full eight hours' rest.

Deep into the night, my dreams of a wonderful future were abruptly shattered by the thunderous roar of incoming rockets and the thump of exploding 82mm mortars. In one motion I slipped on the radio and grabbed my rifle. "Gooks in the wire!" an anonymous voice yelled from a bunker to our right as the crackle of rifle fire echoed all around the base. The air was suddenly filled with the flashes from exploding ordnance and red tracer rounds that cut across the black night. From outside the wire, directly across from us, the flash of an RPG lit up the dark night and sent a screaming projectile splashing into the side of the bunker to our left. Muzzle flashes on the other side of the wire looked like an enormous swarm of fireflies.

When the rocket hit the bunker to our left, I was jolted by the thought that the NVA would try to breach the perimeter right in front of us. Then a flare broke overhead and I saw about fifty enemy soldiers crawling low in the wire while a large force just behind peppered the bunkers with ferocious gunfire. From somewhere in the chaos to the left, a bangalore torpedo blew a large hole in the wire and another rocket crashed into the bunker. A big group of enemy soldiers rushed through the hole in the wire with their guns blazing. We fired furiously at what seemed like an unstoppable tide, trying desperately to plug the hole left by the demolished bunker.

Claymore mines exploded, heavy weapons fired back and forth across a short distance, flares went off here and there, and bullets zipped through the air with great intensity. Two tanks and a platoon of Marines pulled up behind us and fired furiously at the breach in the wire. The enemy soldiers pulled back faster than they'd advanced. Far down the line to the right, an even bigger enemy force punched through the outer defenses in the same way. The situation was so chaotic that it was hard to tell what was going on, which was the main penetration point and which was the diversion.

Even with the tanks to cover them, the platoon that came to our trench found it difficult to move when they tried to shift right toward the other hole in the lines. Heavy machine guns just beyond the wire raked the trenches and bunkers, making any movement very hazardous. Deafening fire in rapid succession from the tanks struck at the forest across from us in an attempt to knock out the machine guns.

As the platoon pulled out, the sergeant in charge ordered us to retake the bunker that had been knocked out by the NVA, but Lane told everyone to stay in the trench. Suddenly, I heard loud Vietnamese voices, then saw silhouettes again rush the bunker to the left. The air was so thick with bullets that it was the greatest hazard to raise our heads above the trench, but if we didn't, the Vietnamese would soon step on our faces. I switched my rifle to full automatic, emptied a clip into the swarm of darting figures just a few yards ahead, then threw both of my grenades.

When too many in the squad had ducked below the top of the trench, Lane and I yelled for them to give it everything they had. I wanted to run, but yelling encouragements to the others also inflated my resolution. Everyone endangered his personal safety in a determined effort to hold back death for all. If every man did not give all he had, we would be overrun.

Enemy troops fired at us from over and around the bunker. When a green tracer round struck the dirt in front of us, I shouted for everyone to "Duck!" A tremendous explosion went off in front of the trench. It was like getting hit in the head with a hammer. My God, we're all gonna die, I thought, then fired my last few bullets. The line held and the enemy troops again pulled away.

All the guys clamored for ammunition; most were completely out. I tried to hush them, in the illogical fear that the enemy would hear and learn our vulnerability. If they came at us again, we could do nothing to stop them. Incoming mortars exploded all around our trench, raising a cloud of dust and smoke. At least I knew that the enemy troops would not assault us during the barrage. Douglas and Lemon ran through the explosions to the position to the right and came back with two cases of M-16 ammunition and two LAWs. As we passed the ammo from hand to hand, we looked at each other with the full realization that some among us would be dead before this thing was over.

The Vietnamese again assaulted the perimeter, but fortunately for us, they struck at the position far to our right. In front of us, a large group of troops still fired in our direction from beyond what was left of the wire. Each time a green tracer round hit at a position, a thunderous explosion soon followed. Marines in the bunkers to our immediate right fell back to the trench when the fronts of their bunkers were blasted with some kind of heavy weapon.

From out of nowhere, a small group of NVA soldiers swept around the back of the bunker just abandoned by the Marines who came to our trench. We focused our fire in that direction, chasing some of the enemy troops into the bunker, then Hunter fired a LAW into the back of the bunker, sending up a spray of debris. It was not another attempt at a breakthrough, just sappers trying to cause havoc behind the first line of defense. Instead, it was they who got sapped. We were still shooting at the bunker when other Marines started to retake it. Only then did I try to communicate with the men to the right by using the radio. But their frequency had changed recently, so I wasn't able to contact them.

Another Delta Company platoon came to us from the darkness behind. After a brief inquiry about enemy strength in our sector, the platoon commander ordered us to join the assault to retake the bunker to our right. Lane

told him that the attacks had been shifting from left to
right and that it was best we stay where we were and protect the flank. The young lieutenant said we had to come
along with his platoon. As we climbed out of the trench
to follow, Lane told us to hold our position. They retook
the bunker very easily, the sappers having already left.
The green tracer rounds hit at the bunker and a flurry of
rockets exploded in the midst of the Marines who were
there. The platoon quickly pulled back to the trench
line behind the bunkers and returned fire. There was
no reason to retake the bunker if the perimeter was
unbroken. A duster pulled up and showered the adjacent
enemy troops with sparks of red metal. It would not last
long in such an exposed position if the North Vietnamese
decided to take it out. To the right of us, the trench was
filled with frightened Marines, truck drivers, engineers,
and anyone else who could hold a rifle.

The two groups exchanged fire across the short distance between the bunker and the trench. Realizing that if
the enemy broke through, we would be trapped, I urged
Lane to pull the squad back, but again he said we'd stay
in the trench. Suddenly, the duster blew up, then sappers
hurled satchel charges at the trench line. The sappers
charged toward the trench just behind the big explosions,
but because the trench was laid out in a zigzag, Marines
on both sides of the point of attack cut the sappers to
pieces. Just as that happened, a flare ship arrived overhead and lit the night sky with bright flares that made our
fire much more effective. I was startled by the sight of
two dead NVA soldiers only a few feet in front of our
trench. Hunter fired a few more shots into them, but I
cautioned him to stop for fear that they carried explosives. The enemy was inside the wire at a few places and
a few bunkers were destroyed, but at no place had the
defenses completely broken down. With the battlefield
awash in light, the enemy's heavy weapons took a
beating, without which they had little chance to crack the

defenses. While there was still darkness to cover them, the enemy finally started to withdraw.

About the same time the enemy started to pull away, Bravo Company came down from C2 in an attempt to trap them against Cam Lo. In the first light of early dawn, the lead element of Bravo made contact with the last enemy unit to leave Cam Lo, but hardly slowed them down in their retreat to the northeast. For those at Cam Lo, the fight that began about two in the morning was finally over.

At first light the ferocity of the battle was apparent to everyone. The air carried the smell of death. Littered along the packed ground between the wire and the bunkers were 150 dead NVA, and another twenty were found badly wounded but alive. Bravo Company made it back to Cam Lo in the early afternoon, bringing another ten prisoners with them, only one of whom was in good enough shape to walk. The weak and injured enemy soldiers had sacrificed themselves to allow the main force to escape. The large number of weapons left behind by the enemy suggested that other dead and wounded were carried away in the hasty withdrawal. The ugly black barrel of a 75mm recoilless rifle stared at us from a position directly across from the bunker to the left. More than two battalions of enemy troops from the 324B Division had failed to break into Cam Lo.

Remarkably, for this great triumph, the Marines had suffered only six dead and thirteen wounded. Everyone in our little squad made it through the night without a scratch, yet there were no happy faces among us. I felt especially bad. Killing and maiming each other seemed a foolish and degenerate enterprise, and the action caused me to doubt myself as a soldier. That doubt was the whole purpose of the Tet Offensive, which struck Washington and Peoria with far greater impact than Cam Lo.

By the time Bravo Company returned to Cam Lo, everyone had gotten his fill of looking at stacks of dead men, and they were buried in the usual way, in a common grave scooped out by a bulldozer. Lieutenant Proust jauntily displayed the prisoners like game trophies, delaying their treatment so that he could have someone take pictures of him standing in front of them. After he relinquished his prizes to intelligence officers, he tried to substitute a big captured .30 caliber machine gun, but Captain Ross canceled his order to take the gun back to C2 and sent us on our way. On the march back to C2, I could hardly put one foot in front of the other; my body was exhausted from long hours of tension. What was supposed to have been a restful night turned out to be one of the most draining.

Chapter 16

Not much happened along the DMZ in the weeks following the Tet Offensive. There were the usual artillery duels, and Delta Company took one KIA and one WIA in yet another ambush along the road, but for the most part there was very little action. The lethargy was broken on February 15, when our platoon went on a patrol to the southwest of Con Thien. The lieutenant was about to march us across another abandoned rice paddy when someone spotted movement ahead. Enemy troops were hustling into position to ambush us as we crossed the rice paddy. While still more than three hundred yards away from the enemy, Lieutenant Proust ordered us to open fire in an attempt to pin them down while he walked in artillery from behind them. The first squad had already started to move into position for us to swing around and attack from the flank. After a quick volley of rifle fire, we retreated, perplexed by our commander's strange orders. We knew there was no chance of the enemy staying in place once we fired on them, and wondered why the lieutenant thought they would just sit around and wait for artillery to blow them to pieces. We could either attack or call in artillery, not both.

When we opened up on the enemy, they sent back only a few shots in return and quickly withdrew. As we pulled back, Lieutenant Proust fumbled with his map and radio, calling long seven-digit coordinates instead of using reference points. By the time the first WP round impacted in the target area, the enemy troops were long gone. The lieutenant bragged about the accuracy of his OF efforts, unaware that the shells destroyed only flora.

After the brief barrage, we moved through the other side of the rice paddy; only the lieutenant expected to find anyone there. After we passed through the target area, the lieutenant halted the platoon abruptly and gave a panicked call to the company CP about fifteen enemy soldiers crossing a ridge approximately five hundred yards away. Even I, who had become accustomed to his peculiarities, was puzzled as I watched him scramble for coordinates on the map. Not only did no one else see the supposed enemy soldiers, but we could see no more than two hundred yards in front of us. Just the same, a single Skyhawk swooped low on the phantom target, strafing and bombing an imaginary enemy as we trotted away from the scene. A patrol from Con Thien went to check the results of the bombing while we headed to C2.

Back at the base there were nothing but sullen faces all around the platoon. Not only had our platoon commander almost walked us into an ambush, but once the enemy was discovered, he allowed them to escape unhurt. One of the few times when we had the numerical and tactical advantage, and the idiot squandered it.

"Someone is going to have to pull his coat about this walkin' across rice paddies shit," Lemon suggested.

"We gonna have to do more than that before he gets somebody killed," Wallace said.

"Somebody is gonna have to do him," I said, articulating the obvious conclusion around which they skirted. A small group of conspirators, mainly the squad leaders, gathered in a bunker near the south gate to decide what should be done. Lieutenant Proust must die, was the consensus quickly reached, and all discussion focused on how it was to be accomplished. It was suggested we hire an assassin to do the job, as had happened in Delta Company when, in a situation similar to ours, the platoon commander of a disgruntled group was shot in the head while checking the perimeter. Brecht knew who had arranged that murder and offered to contact the killer so we could do the same. It sounded like a good idea until he told us the approximate cost of the arrangement. We decided that we should kill him ourselves.

We were in the midst of hatching a plot when Flash came into the bunker and summoned the squad leaders to the company CP. There was no fear that the murder plot had been discovered. A thousand people could know about something like that and it would never get back to the authorities. The squad leaders came rushing back to the platoon with word for everyone to saddle up. About four miles to the northeast, a helicopter had been shot down while attempting to extract a reconnaissance team from a small clearing. The second platoon, already out on patrol, hurried toward the call for help.

After waiting for about an hour for helicopters that did not come, we headed into the twilight at a very fast forced march. As the second platoon closed in on the downed helicopter, they came under heavy enemy fire near the top of a small hill. After shooting their way to the top of the hill, the second platoon circled into a defensive perimeter and waited for help to arrive from the rest of the company. A half hour passed, with them taking only a few shots and a few grenades. Confident that they hadn't walked into a trap, the Marines continued through the light enemy resistance, cutting a path through the heavy brush with blazing fire from M-60 machine guns.

In the meantime, the rest of the company struggled through difficult terrain, ineptly directed through deep gullies and thick undergrowth. In the dark of night, concealment in the brush was not as critical as during the day, yet we battered our way along a difficult route when much quicker and easier paths were available. That kind of ineptitude was inexcusable when the lives of the Marines at the downed helicopter might very well depend on how quickly we reached them.

When the second platoon came close to the overturned helicopter, they were again fired on by a small enemy force. In the sporadic shooting, Hebert, the platoon radio operator, was hit in the head and chest and killed instantly. Four other Marines were slightly wounded in the close-quarter firefight. The platoon quickly formed another defensive circle near the wrecked helicopter and sent a search party to check for survivors.

Outside the helicopter lay two dead NVA soldiers, their wounds still dripping blood. "Five Marines, all dead," someone from the search party called out from inside the helicopter.

From the heap of bloody corpses an angry voice responded, "I'm not dead, you idiot!" A badly wounded crewman lay beneath the bodies of our dead Marines. He told of how the helicopter was swarmed over by enemy soldiers who stripped it of everything they could carry away, including the watch from his wrist as he played dead. More important, he said that some of the recon team had escaped into the bush.

High above the wreckage, a C-130 dropped a steady stream of flares, which allowed the second platoon to search for the missing men who might be lying wounded somewhere nearby. Following the beacon of light left by the flare ship, we closed within five hundred yards of the second platoon, then circled into a defensive perimeter of our own to wait out the night.

At dawn the next morning we joined them in a search for the men still missing. Individual squads radiated out from the helicopter in all directions, each silently hoping that the missing Marines had found hiding places in the thick brush. Soon after we'd covered the area closer to the helicopter, shots rang out. A bullet cut across the back of Hunter, slicing at his fleshy muscles like a meat cleaver.

Lane drove the rest of the squad toward the sound of the shots in a fast-moving column, coordinating the movement with Frost as we went. We linked up while on the move and swept through the bush without finding anyone. On the way back to the helicopter, Clark spotted something rustling in the bushes across a wide clearing. The squad fell into position to fire at whoever came into the clearing. A man in a tiger-striped uniform stumbled out into the clearing.

"Hold your fire!" I shouted before anyone could cut down the distant figure. It was one of the missing members of the Force Recon team, fleeing desperately from sound that he apparently thought was made by the enemy. Though psychologically shocked, he was otherwise all right. In his dazed and frightened state, he led us to a place where he'd last seen the other missing member of the recon team. The successful conclusion of one search lifted our spirits and hopes that the other man could also be found alive.

While sweeping back and forth through the bush near the last known hiding place of the missing man, I made a gruesome discovery that ended our search. There, lying in the grass, was my friend Bryan Whitehead, the back of his head blown off by a bullet that entered his forehead. I squatted beside him and pushed his brain back into what was left of his skull. I was devastated as never before. Whitehead had walked the same streets that I had, went to the same movie theaters, and we'd shared a common attitude about so many things. A heavy weight of depression fell over me as I wondered why it hadn't been someone else who discovered him. I sat in the grass and put together pieces of a skull fragment like working a jigsaw puzzle, then tucked them under flaps of scalp and tied it all together with a battle dressing. Half in a daze, we lifted him onto a makeshift stretcher of ponchos, his body already hard with rigor mortis. After the dead and wounded were picked up, the wrecked helicopter was set ablaze with magnesium grenades and we returned to C2.

As soon as we got back to the base, we were battered by a pounding of more than a hundred 152mm shells. These very big shells were extremely dangerous, able to knock down the strongest bunker. Yet we suffered only shaken nerves from the big barrage.

The next day was a nice change from the cumbersome company-size excursions in which we had mainly operated since our return north. In teams of four or five men, we patrolled around the base in all directions, just protecting the road at first, but later the radius of operation pushed far away from the base. I liked working in small teams, since your fortunes or misfortunes were more of your own making, and the degree of skill required was higher, rather than simply being a chance happening or the consequences of some imprudent decision. If I took a bullet in the head because of some stupid mistake, the mistake would most likely be my own.

It was about noon on February 27 when Frost, Colletta, Douglas, and I stealthily made our way along in one of these small patrols. At about three miles out, the heavy thump of a .50 caliber machine gun sent us sinking into the grass. It was not shooting at us, but at a bird dog that buzzed over the Ben Hai River. About three hundred yards from us, we could clearly see puffs of smoke rise from the concealed position of the heavy machine gun. Happy at our discovery, we slipped away in the direction from which we'd come and called in an artillery mission on the unsuspecting enemy. We did not go to check the results of the bombardment, because we thought it unlikely the machine gun was out there all alone. Our assumption, it happened, was correct. A patrol team the same size as ours had ventured far to the northeast of Cam Lo. The Delta Company Marines, hearing voices along a trail, hastily took cover where they could.

Only thirty feet ahead of them a platoon of NVA troops stepped onto the trail. The small group of Marines opened up with all they had, shooting furiously at point-blank range, then quickly making a run for C1. Our platoon responded quickly, searching the area of the fire-fight for any NVA who might still be around. Eight dead enemy troops were found sprawled about the trail, but no one else.

The small patrol teams became so productive that they were used more frequently than at any time in the past, and covered more territory. I volunteered to go on one of the deep penetration patrols led by Sergeant Wilson. Lightly provisioned, we were to cover about twenty miles in two days, marching through enemy-infested territory. I was unsure of Sergeant Wilson's stamina and resolve as we headed east into the brush-covered hills. At about eight miles out we came upon signs that someone had recently passed through the area. Grass was trampled down, twigs on bushes were broken in one direction, there were even some splotches of betel nut, which the Vietnamese liked to chew.

Slowly and carefully we crept toward our first check-point, an abandoned village. Our planned route called for us to go around the southern edge of the village, but Sergeant Wilson decided to go to the north to take advantage of the thicker foliage in that direction. Close to the village, we came across fresh footprints. I called the finding back to C2 as we crouched so low that we were almost crawling. I stepped, heel first, then rolling the outer edge until the toe was down, then laying the foot flat, finally shifting the weight forward. The crunch of grass and snap of twigs were muffled in this slow method of walking. This is how Bryan must have died, I thought as we moved in the footsteps of the enemy.

At the head of the short column, Hines stopped and slowly lay flat in the tall weeds. The electricity in his body told us that our suspicions had been correct. Not even risking a whisper, Hines held up five fingers and flashed them four times, signifying a platoon of enemy soldiers. Without chancing even a deep breath, we watched the NVA troops busily move about the edge of the village.

An hour passed, but still they were so close that we dared not move an eyelash. Discovery was almost certain death. After about three hours the NVA troops started to move out. I gripped my rifle and swallowed my fear as two columns of enemy troops came straight toward us. They chattered casually and laughed with each other as they came closer. I prayed to God that we would not be seen, but felt I was at the moment of death. The swish of their pants legs in the grass was more like the sound of an old steam locomotive. They passed no more than twenty feet from us. Even after they were gone, I still heard the shadows of their footsteps. Four NVA soldiers who remained in the village covered up something near a hedgerow, then left in the same direction as the others.

We waited a long time for the enemy soldiers to return, the minutes passing like hours, then, on legs still shaky with fear, Sergeant Wilson and I crept into the village to see what the enemy had left behind. In a hole beneath the leaves and bushes, we found an old .30 caliber machine gun wrapped in cloth. Sergeant Wilson lifted the machine gun out of the shallow hole and handed it to me, then reached down for the cans of ammunition that were also there. Suddenly, a shot jolted the gun from my hands. From the direction that the enemy platoon had left, a single enemy stood cranking bullets our way. No more than twenty feet from the NVA soldier, Hines stood and shot him in the head, flipping his pith helmet high in the air.

Sergeant Wilson and I fired at the already dead enemy, striking another enemy soldier whom we did not see until he was shot. Hines and Colletta ran toward us, spraying the bush behind them. Another NVA soldier foolishly broke from the brush and fired at us, a mistake for which he paid with his life.

I looked all around, expecting the enemy to come at us from any direction, at the same time I transmitted a sit-rep of how hot things had become. With the old sergeant leading the way, we ran out of the village in no particular direction, guided only by brush that offered the least resistance. A few hundred yards away Sergeant Wilson stumbled to a halt, winded. Colletta was as white as snow and even more winded. Reminding them of the recently departed enemy platoon, I urged them to get moving.

Getting our bearings, we headed west because Sergeant Wilson figured the NVA would try to cut us off from the base. The rest of the platoon was ready to come to our rescue, but Sergeant Wilson assured the CP that we'd eluded the enemy. The village, a well-known feature on everyone's map, was pounded with artillery even though we had not called for a mission. After walking in a wide loop, we returned to the base from the south late in the night, a full day ahead of schedule.

Before morning arrived, we were again en route to the village along with the rest of the company. Marching a very difficult path, we reached the village just before sunrise. With scouts ahead, the company spread out and moved through all parts of the village at the same time. The only enemy soldiers found were those we'd killed the previous day. In addition to the old machine gun that saved my life, we found two M-60 mortar tubes with twenty rounds of ammunition, ten medical kits, two RPGs with twenty rounds of ammunition, and a thousand rounds of 7.62 ammunition. I walked over, took a long look at the two dead men who had tried to kill me, and searched them for papers or something that would make them more than just hunks of dead meat, but there was nothing. As the company headed back to C2, we left them there to rot in the hot tropical sun. I was very tense during the march and did not relax until Route 561 came into view; that is, I relaxed about as much as you could in Vietnam. As we approached the base, I was seeing flashes of light out of the corners of my eyes, not artillery or gunfire, but hallucination brought on by fatigue and sleep deprivation.

The small patrols were good tactics so long as they were not overused. If the NVA caught on, as they surely would, it was only a matter of time before at least one of the small patrols would be wiped out. There would soon be hunter teams of enemy troops roaming the DMZ with no other purpose than to find the small patrols and destroy them one by one.

It looked as if the enemy had wised up very quickly, because the number of sightings by the small patrols dropped off dramatically in the days that followed. A group from Delta Company that patrolled west of Route 561, just south of C2, spotted a single enemy soldier as he closed the hatch of a spider trap. Suspecting that the solitary enemy soldier was bait to pull them into an ambush, the Marines called in artillery. Frightened by the artillery, which exploded behind him, the enemy soldier popped up out of the hole to run and was immediately shot to death. In the surrounding brush the Marines found the mutilated bodies of ten other enemy soldiers. On the same day, the first platoon from our company caught another group of would-be ambushers and killed five of them. The picture was clear, the enemy was now after the small patrols. When they got a whole platoon instead, it was more than they could handle.

The enemy responded by shifting more mortar fire and H&I to areas surrounding the base rather than on the base itself, inhibiting the movement of large units. However, long-range enemy artillery continued to make C2 a dangerous place to be. Big 130mm shells fired from more than 5,600 meters away struck directly atop one of the bunkers in our platoon's section of the line, severely wounding Ducart and Flash. On that sorrowful note, February ended.

Chapter 17

The beginning of March saw the resurrection of Operation Kentucky, a project that sent our company far to the southwestern corner of the DMZ to act as a blocking force for a sweep conducted by the Ninth Marines. The operation gave us some exposure to territory we'd never seen, but did not bring any contact with the enemy. Soon after we returned to C2, Lieutenant Proust, Abbot, and Hunter went on one of the small patrols. At about 0300 they stopped on a grassy knoll that gave them a good view of the surrounding area. Before they were completely set up for an LP, more than two companies of NVA troops came out of the ground like nocturnal gophers, some of them not more than ten feet from the frightened Marines. It looked as though luck had finally run out for small patrols.

With the handset of the radio buried deep in the soft part of his abdomen, Abbot dared not try to make a report of the situation. Right near them, an enemy soldier dug a latrine into which a steady stream of troops relieved themselves. It was only a matter of time before someone stumbled upon them. The shitters stopped coming, the dogs stopped barking, and the night grew quiet. When the sun rose, the enemy troops were gone. The knoll was littered with Chieu Hoi leaflets—"Open Arms," i.e., invitations to take part in an amnesty program—used as toilet paper. The Marines had stumbled into a bivouac area for enemy troops moving south. All around were heavily fortified earthen bunkers covered with grass to make them look like all the other grassy knolls in the area.

A few minutes after Abbot made a report of their startling discovery, a bird dog swooped low over the trees in search of the recently departed enemy soldiers. To the surprise of the small group of Marines, other NVA soldiers came out of the bunkers and fired at the small plane. The message came from the company CP for the patrol team to get out of the area as quickly as possible so that all the bases in the area could fire artillery into the enemy camp. Abbot was so frustrated by the order that he cursed in acknowledgment. Here was a grand opportunity to catch a large group of enemy soldiers off guard, and our leaders were going to let them know that the camp had been discovered by shooting a lot of artillery into the area.

The area was ripe for ambush or some kind of trap, but instead planes were flying overhead and artillery was pounding the enemy compound, all alerting them to the fact that their hiding place had been discovered. Lieutenant Proust suggested that the camp might still be ripe for ambush because enemy troops had come out of the bunkers and fired at the bird dog, thus giving away the camp's location.

"Are you kidding?" I said. "That plane could have gotten shot at from Gio Linh to Lang Vei."

The following day the Ninth Marines swept through the area and found a labyrinth of bunkers and tunnels, but of course, no enemy soldiers.

Back at C2, Abbot, normally the typical composed New Englander, talked on and on about how they were inches from death, camped in the middle of an NVA battalion. "It was like being in a swimming pool with a school of great white sharks," he said. He joked that he could go home and brag that he was once in the North Vietnamese Army.

"You'll be a real cool John Wayne back in that little hick town," Colletta said slowly.

That sent Gutierrez into a long and funny recollection. "I once saw John Wayne waste Mexicans all day long. He was killin' Mexicans on the TV early in the morning, and when I came home that evening, he was still kickin' Mexican butts." We all laughed. For the next few days all conversation was dominated by talk of the mishandling of the discovery of the enemy camp and the use of small patrols.

On March 6 we again thought time had run out on the small patrols when we got a call for help from an Alpha Company unit. While on patrol to the southwest of Con Thien, a six-man unit of Marines spotted eight NVA soldiers moving away from them. The Marines tried to call in artillery on the heavily camouflaged enemy, but by the time they got the mission cleared, the NVA troops were out of sight. The Marines immediately went in pursuit of the enemy, hoping to move in close and yet preserve their advantage of surprise.

They marched about a thousand yards before again spotting the enemy troops. With only three hundred yards between them, the Marines opened up on their quarry. Much to their consternation, not only did the enemy ahead of them return fire, but so did a larger group of enemy soldiers from an adjacent position. The Marines continued to move toward their original target, the path of least resistance. They desperately called for artillery to throw up a barrier between them and the larger enemy force. Because they had tried to call in artillery only a short time earlier, 105 rounds quickly impacted on target and dissuaded enemy troops from coming up the small hill on which the Marines took refuge. The eight NVA soldiers who started the fray closed in too soon, and without the help of the larger group, their number was quickly reduced to four by the fierce defense the Marines put up.

Our platoon was out of C2 along with the first artillery shells, marching at breakneck speed in a direct route toward the besieged Marines. In the meantime, the Alpha Company unit tried to get off the hill and head east, but was prevented by enemy troops who encircled them, two of the Marines being wounded. The leader of the small group of Marines had one eye gone and his cheekbone shattered. He knew his team had no chance of holding back the much larger enemy that the artillery onslaught had temporarily halted. When a large group of NVA soldiers charged up the hill from the east, the Marines had no choice but to flee in the opposite direction. Two more Marines were wounded as they got to the bottom of the hill but were able to find temporary concealment in a thicket of brush. The radio operator adjusted artillery fire onto the top of the hill, causing the hard-charging enemy to change his route.

Ahead of our rather noisy approach, the NVA faded into the bush to the north, leaving behind only three men to cover their withdrawal. The enemy trio was very effective, stopping our entire platoon at the top of the hill and even causing us to momentarily withdraw in an attempt to circumvent their fire. Wallace completely lost his composure and screamed curses at the lieutenant for not maneuvering a squad to one side of the three enemy troops. Separated widely from one another, the three enemy soldiers made no attempt to flee when they had the chance to do so. Directed by Frost, Gutierrez thumped M-79 rounds on top of the courageous trio, killing two and chasing the other away.

Directed by calls over the radio, we found the shot-up Alpha Company patrol team in a clump of brush, all but one badly wounded. Their lives depended on getting to the operating tables as fast as the helicopters could carry them.

Our return to C2 was greeted with the usual long barrage of 130mm shells. Safe inside the biggest and strongest bunker in the platoon area, Abbot and Colletta started a card game, Doc White lay down for a nap, and I started a letter home, all of us carrying on in the most normal way while above us a most abnormal shelling shattered vital equipment and installations. Our complacency was shaken along with the rafters when a big 120mm rocket dug a deep crater at the entrance to our bunker. Between radio watches, sleep was uneasy; the near miss of the rocket was a reminder that death could erupt in thunder and smoke at any moment, that at any moment someone you called a friend could vanish without warning, that at any moment you could become but a memory. Such was life along the DMZ.

On March 9 our company pulled out of C2, headed for a redeployment at a new fire support base with another generic name, A4. About two miles southwest of Con Thien, A4 was a well-constructed base, but its utility was questionable because it was so close to C2 and Con Thien. Because the base was so new, we moved in with few adjustments to be done. While unpacking equipment from the move, a mortar crew from 2/12 accidentally struck a box of primers with some hard object, causing a quick and horrible fire. All four of the men in the mortar pit were badly burned. Their screams of agony brought a swarm of men rushing to their aid. Warning of the danger of further explosions, Sergeant Wilson sent away all but a few of the would-be rescuers. The mortar men were horrible sights, clothes burned, skin a mass of blisters. The air was permeated with the smell of burned hair and flesh. Two of them slipped away into unconsciousness before medevac helicopters arrived. If any of them survived—of course, we never learned—they must have been badly disfigured.

In the late evening of our first day at A4, an OP sighted six NVA soldiers about four hundred yards away and called in 81mm mortars. The notoriously inaccurate mortars uncharacteristically landed right on top of the enemy soldiers, killing four of them with the first explosion and reducing the other two to amputees. As the platoon went out to make sure there were no other enemy troops lurking about, I expected A4 to be as rough and active as C2; however, the days that followed were very quiet. Artillery flew low overhead, headed for a fiery destination in C2. None of the shells fell on A4. Work out of A4 was mainly squad-size patrols, close to the base. Back at C2, a Delta Company LP used a starlight scope to shoot to death four enemy soldiers during the middle of the night. We were at A4 ten days before receiving any attention from the enemy. Early one morning, twenty 152mm shells fell on the base at the rate of one round per minute. After the bombardment by the big guns, we constructed permanently fortified listening posts about two hundred yards north and east of the base.

Brecht and I were the first to pull duty at one of the newly constructed appendages, using it as an OP instead of the LP, as it was intended. We rested comfortably in the shade of bushes at the top of a hill that offered a good view of the distant territory to the northeast as the humid morning passed to a blistering hot afternoon. Across the shimmering heat, I was shocked by the sight of ten NVA soldiers who weaved through waist-high grass in the distance. They appeared and disappeared repeatedly. For a moment I doubted myself, thinking that enemy soldiers would not walk through a field of grass so close to the base during the middle of the day. Then they would reappear.

I snatched the binoculars from Brecht's neck to make sure the distant figures were not lost Marines. While I plotted the location of the grassy field on the map, Brecht spotted three other Vietnamese on the edge of the clearing. "Thirteen hogs at 4D119732 moving south at forty-five degrees," I called to the company CP, trying to be as specific as I could. Though the enemy soldiers were clearly far beyond the effective range of our rifles, Brecht and I fired anyway. Soon after the mortar fire ended, a bird dog appeared over the field. After it left, the grassy field was plastered by a high-altitude air strike. Another pass by the bird dog counted only three enemy dead. Everyone in the platoon got ready to go out and check the grassy field, but no such order came.

With insulting arrogance, seventeen enemy soldiers showed themselves in the grassy field the very next day. If they were going to expose themselves, we were more than happy to kill them. Using 105mm cannons on this kind of artillery mission proved most effective; they got the most coverage on target in the shortest time. By some mysterious method of counting, ten of the enemy soldiers were counted as killed; none of our troops went out to check the results firsthand.

On March 29, Marines at the same OP site once again sighted NVA troops in the grassy field. Targets preplotted and cannons ready, the OP was waiting for them. The enemy soldiers were quickly surrounded with high explosives. But that time, 100mm shells came into A4 as the 105mm shells went out. We could not hear the incoming artillery because of our own cannons, so many people got caught out in the open. Three Marines were severely wounded. Most of us had come to the conclusion that the grassy field was part of an infiltration route, and that NVA troops already in the pipeline would continue to use it until the cost of doing so was too much to pay. It was most probably a camp similar to the one found by the small patrol led by Lieutenant Proust. The whole company was abuzz with rumors that we would soon go out to take possession of the grassy field or to set up some kind of trap for enemy troops who passed through the area. However, our leaders continued to try to interdict the soldiers on the grassy field with artillery. They saw the grassy field as just another part of our total area of operations. We continued our patrols as if that particular area had no special significance.

In the evening of March 29 six more NVA soldiers were moving through the same grassy field. If the NVA kept using the route, enough of them had to be getting through to satisfy the NVA commanders. The people we saw and the people we killed must have been only a small portion of those who passed that way. Neither artillery, nor airpower, nor anything else, could control territory like men on the ground. After all the operations we'd conducted to find enemy troops, it was very frustrating that enemy troops were still close at hand. Even so, we continued to operate in a business-as-usual manner. March ended without us making a challenge for control of the grassy field.

For the first week of April, the northern OP continued to sight enemy soldiers in the grassy field, and still we did not go out to meet them. But at the end of the week, two M-48 tanks came up from Cam Lo to add their very accurate guns to efforts to interdict traffic there. The 90mm guns could put a shell on the target on the first shot, but the 90mm cannon could be most effective because they so easily retrained they were like huge rifles. Still, against troops in the open, the kill radius of the 105mm cannon made it the more effective weapon if it could be brought on the target very quickly. The apparent tactic was to have the tanks pin down the enemy troops until more effective weapons could be used against them.

The next time my turn came around to go out on an OP, I again saw six NVA soldiers in the faraway field. The map I carried already had preplotted coordinates printed in big blue numbers. This made it quick and easy to get a mission on the targets. Tank-fired cannons and .50 caliber machine guns, then big eight-inch howitzers, erupted the whole field into geysers of smoking dust. The NVA responded with one of my favorite tactics, running like hell. They dashed right through the tank fire and only one of the enemy soldiers was killed.

In the days that followed, the NVA seemed to shift

their infiltration route farther to the east, because Gio Linh began to call in frequent sightings. Traditionally, in the eastern DMZ, Con Thien and Gio Linh took the most incoming artillery, but since the bombing halt of November, there seemed to be a lot more artillery shells for everybody. Soon even A4 became a well-worked target of enemy gunners across the river. Moving around in trenches with ears tuned for the sound of incoming shells, we lived the subterranean life that was common to bases along the DMZ. There was no more sleeping under the stars, as we did when we first arrived at the base.

While the NVA streamed southward to our east, our offensive mission continued to be the protection of traffic along the road between Con Thien and Cam Lo. Marching southward along the flanks of the road between A4 and C2, the first platoon spotted movement in the nearby brush. Half the platoon opened up at once, sending the unknown number of enemy troops fleeing in panic. No one was killed, but an ambush was foiled. In a shallow hole concealed by bushes, the enemy soldiers left behind four RPGs and two AK-47s. An attempted ambush so close to the base was very bad news to us, not because the enemy troops had gotten away, but because we knew that when the report reached the battalion CO, we would be kept from the grassy field and ordered to step up duty along the road. Later the same day, NVA were again sighted moving through the grassy field.

Frequent sightings by the OP to the northeast prompted the move of a 106mm recoilless rifle to that location and placing someone at the position around the clock. The next time the enemy appeared in the grassy field, the 106 sent a high-velocity shell slamming into the midst of the dozen men there, cutting their number in half. The low trajectory and high velocity of the 106mm made it perfect for the mission, only its slow rate of fire inhibiting its effectiveness. After the recoilless rifle blasted the enemy troops, an aerial observer circled low over the field, apparently trying to draw enemy fire. If any were still there, they wisely did not shoot at the small plane. Just the same, an F-4 Phantom streaked low in a power dive followed by a string of big explosions.

Late in the morning, patrols were canceled and orders were passed out for everyone to put on helmets and flak jackets and stand by our bunkers. In the wild speculation that followed, we concluded that an offensive operation would be launched to stop the infiltration. Toward noon two Hueys fluttered in from the south and dropped off three generals.

Out stepped the generals with a pack of flunkies in tow, deities come to earth trailing a long line of apostles. Our new company commander, Captain Harris, genuflected and promptly ushered the royal procession into the CP.

"Something really big must be about to happen, look at all them clipboards," Hart said, tongue in cheek. "A clipboard is some heavy-duty shit."

"I guess we gonna be clipboardin' the shit outta them NVA," Lemon chided.

"They might just clipboard our asses right out of existence," I said.

Hart joked that "all of them would get Bronze Stars for coming up here."

We could only speculate as to the identities of our imperial visitors; no one bothered to tell us who they were. Now, could you imagine Patton or Bradley going to some frontline unit without speaking so much as a syllable to the troops? To them, we were just parts of the machine, no different from cannons or jeeps. We were superfluous; they were there to fill their clipboards. Apparently, nobody wanted to stop the infiltration, because it resulted in a steady stream of favorable statistics, a couple dozen kills a week at very little cost. That looked good for everybody, and might even mean promotions for the lower-ranking officers. But down in the ranks, those of us with our faces in the mud knew that kind of thinking was not going to win the war.

I explained it to Lane this way: "Let's say that you're an NVA commander in the Cam Lo area and you need ten men a week. If you know that three will be killed along the infiltration route, you just order thirteen. That's what's happening out on the grassy field. If we could kill, say, five out of that ten, they would find some other place to go most ricky tick." Really safe places to go along the DMZ were rare, so the NVA continued to use established routes as long as the cost was not too high.

Later on that day, OP2 again saw enemy troops near the grassy field, eleven soldiers in camouflage uniforms weaving through the tall grass and thin bush on the eastern side of the clearing. Again an AO circled overhead, again an F-4 Phantom streaked low and dropped bombs, and still we just watched.

Chapter 18

On April 10, two platoons from 3/3 arrived at A4 and were integrated into the line. We expected that their arrival would free our company to attack and ambush enemy troops passing to the east. Instead we just marched up and down the road. It got to the point where some of us were even seriously talking about sneaking out to ambush the enemy who so frequently passed so close. When OP2 saw five NVA soldiers pick up the bodies of those killed the previous day, Lieutenant Proust had to threaten Wallace with court-martial to keep him from taking his squad into the field. The lieutenant's harshness resurrected talk of his murder, but in the meantime there were more important conspiracies to be attended.

Later that night a small group met in a bunker to develop a plan that would force offensive operations into the grassy field. The conspirators hatched several plots before settling on one in which a patrol was to flee from a substantial enemy force, forcing the patrol far off course and into the grassy field. There, the enemy would catch up with the squad and pin it down. The rest of the company would then be forced to come to the rescue. The plan required the agreement and cooperation of a great many people. For several days the plot was primed with false reports of large groups of enemy soldiers who suddenly vanished in the field of grass. Then came the opportunity, a patrol of two squads east of the road that was to go all the way to C2.

Nineteen of us involved in the patrol met and agreed that we would go through with the plot. Over and over, I tried to make sure everyone was aware that if we were successful, someone would most likely get killed. But it seemed that no one was there just to survive—or maybe we all just thought that "it" would happen to someone else. The biggest danger in the conspiracy was that we could be hit by friendly fire.

Out in the middle of the patrol, we again stopped to confer with each other. If any one person objected to perpetrating the fraud, we would continue along the prescribed route; the guys were not just willing, they were anxious to get on with it. As we started out to the east, I called in a sit-rep that we'd spotted a small group of enemy soldiers and were in hot pursuit. Captain Harris told me to get some artillery on them and get back to the route. I told him they were too close and that we did not have them in sight at the moment. We walked briskly toward the field for another half hour, about as much time as we thought we could get away with, on the premise of hot pursuit, then sprang the big one. I screamed a panicked message into the radio that we were being attacked by a platoon or more of NVA troops while the guys fired their rifles to provide the appropriate background noise.

Our new company commander stepped right into our subterfuge by ordering us to get out of the area as fast as we could so artillery could hammer the area. With shells exploding on a false target behind us, we moved eastward as fast as we could. Still, it took about two hours of marching to come parallel with the grassy field. The topography began a gentle roll as we swung northward toward the object of our ruse. Playing the part of a ship blown off course by a sudden storm, I made sure we were not mistaken for the enemy by communicating directly with as many units as I could instead of just relying on the company CP to coordinate the information.

Close up, the "flat field of grass" turned out to be a

bumpy cluster of grass-covered mounds, and it was at least twice as large as it looked from the OP site. Between the mounds was a web of tunnels and trenches, all covered with grass, through which a whole battalion could pass without being seen. So then why did some of the troops cross the tops of the mounds where they could be seen? That was a question for which we had no answer.

Brecht spotted an earthen bunker near the top of one of the mounds on the edge of the clearing. Our aggressive anticipation changed to wide-eyed fear in realization that our lies could come true. All those bunkers, all those trenches, it looked very bad; the terrain started to close in around us. More than one person suggested we turn back. Wallace and Frost readily agreed, saying it would take far more men than we had in our little group to explore the fortifications. We, who had risked so much to get to the grassy field, were very glad to head back to A4. On the way, we came across a row of tall aiming sticks that looked like surveying rods and took them back to the base for intelligence observation. A report of what we found in the field made an operation in the area unavoidable.

Once the field had been penetrated, our commanders seemed far more willing to send Marines into the area. Delta Company was the first to direct an offensive operation specifically at the region, and while its men crossed the mounds, on the edge of the field unseen enemy soldiers fired about thirty rifle shots at them, then followed with a blast from a B-40 RPG, none of which caused any casualties. The enemy did not stand and fight in the NVA fashion, but faded away like Viet Cong. In their search for the enemy who'd fired the shots, the Marines found sixteen NVA corpses neatly stacked in a long trench. The company brushed along the outer fringes of the field, then headed for C2.

As they did so, we made preparations for the long-overdue operation to take control of the grassy field. The following day our company invaded from the west and Alpha Company from the north. Unlike our first probe into the field, we were full of confidence and anxious to get into a fight, yet no enemy contested our presence. In the scrub forest to the north, Alpha Company found a bivouac area capable of sheltering a large enemy force, twenty-four large bunkers, two large circular antiaircraft positions, trenches, and tunnels. High in a tree above the camp, an observation platform offered good views of C2 and A4. Numerous shallow graves around the camp told us that the former tenants did not always have a pleasant stay. Fourteen of the graves were uncovered to make sure they contained bodies and not weapons. The putrid stench of rotting bodies in various stages of decay followed us for miles when we left the area and headed back to the base.

There was considerable debate about whether or not the camp had been used by a large group of NVA. Many contended that there were a few signs of large-scale occupation, while others said the volume of junk found underground was proof enough. If the NVA built an area that could hold a battalion, they would surely put a battalion in it. There was hope of solving the mystery after Delta Company had a small but important firefight on the southern edge of the grassy field. A platoon of Marines shot up a squad of NVA soldiers, killing two of them while sustaining only one wounded themselves.

However, the most important outcome of the fight was that one enemy soldier was captured alive. The captive was in danger of losing one leg, but his mouth was in good shape, so he could be interrogated right away. To induce him to answer questions, the platoon commander stopped the medic from working on the man's wounded leg. He answered most fluidly. The captive was then bound and blindfolded, and shipped out to Dong Ha for more extensive questioning by ARVN authorities. He lay side by side with the Marine who was wounded in the same fight, as the both of them were placed aboard a medevac helicopter.

When our platoon once again patrolled through the grassy field, we took along engineers to blow up bunkers and other fortifications. In the wooded area on the western edge of the field, we stopped to allow engineers to set explosive charges in a string of bunkers. We moved to a safe distance and the first of the seven bunkers went up in smoke. Suddenly, shots came at us from the other side of the explosions, and eight NVA soldiers dashed away across the top of one of the mounds. Another one of the bunkers blew up. We fired at them furiously but could not pursue because of the explosions in the bunkers between us. When the chain of explosions was finally over, we swept the mound and found two dead enemy soldiers. Instead of going in search of the six who got away, we continued destroying bunkers and tunnels until the engineers had used up all of their C-4 (a plastic explosive), then circled back into the bush.

Patrols along the road continued to have top priority over all other types. Because our ventures into the grassy field had yielded so little action, the size of the units operating in the area was scaled down from platoons to squads. Two days after our platoon had blown up the bunkers and tunnels, a squad from Alpha Company returned to the bivouac complex north of the field on a similar mission. Marines were sowing explosive charges through a string of bunkers and trenches when a storm of gunfire erupted from a nearby bunker. Three Marines were cut down, badly wounded but alive. Dragging their wounded with them, the heavily armed squad quickly plunged into a trench and fired back with everything they had. Behind a torrent of gunfire, the large enemy force threatened to sweep over the Marines like an unstoppable tidal wave, held back only by big explosions that were meant to destroy bunkers.

While the Marines gave full attention to the enemy no

more than fifty yards to their front, other NVA soldiers circled around to one flank and opened fire. A bullet tore off the back of the squad leader's head, dropping him in a lump. Another bullet smashed into the back of the grenadier, leaving him paralyzed and near death. The Marines turned back the enemy on the flank as well, but not before another in their ranks was killed from multiple chest wounds. Then the Marines fired six well-placed LAWs into the enemy bunkers, taking some of the steam out of the enemy's firepower. The Vietnamese responded by hurling grenades, one of which exploded in the trench and badly wounded three men. With half their number out of action, the Marines had no hope of holding back the NVA soldiers if they decided to assault the trench.

Their commanders apparently as conservative as ours, the NVA unit was content to envelop the Marines and pour down bullets upon them. Anchored down by dead and wounded, the Marines still could not attempt to break out of the trap, they could only die together. It looked as if the squad would be wiped out; however, the enemy's conservative tactics allowed time for a platoon from Alpha Company to reach the area. The Marines rushed forward in an uninhibited advance, the muzzle flashes of their weapons searching the grass and brush like beacons in a fog. The NVA troops reeled backward and took up defensive positions in the bivouac area. The Marines divided and attacked from two different positions. One-half of the Marines ran into a whole company of NVA troops who were on their way to rescue their friends. The platoon joined together again and quickly backpedaled to the grassy field. The two groups fired at each other through a patchwork of sunlight and shadows, each maneuvering for some tactical advantage.

When it was discovered that most of the NVA troops had circled around to one side to try an envelopment, the Marines pushed straight ahead into the bivouac area, avoiding a trap and putting pressure on the enemy there.

To stop the Marines from overrunning the camp, the NVA threw yet another company of troops into the fight. Again the Marines pulled back to the grassy field, but now the way out was blocked by the troops who tried the envelopment. In the chaos of the very fluid fight, some of the opposing sides were as close as twenty-five feet. The Marine platoon tried to punch through the eastern side of the grassy field, but the enemy troops had closed the loop and had them trapped. Already out on patrol, a platoon from Delta Company rushed to the aid of the encircled Marines and crashed into the southern side of the grassy field. The NVA suddenly found they were spread too thin and shifted to consolidate their forces. As they did, the Marines joined forces and battled their way into the forest camp once again, jumping into holes and trenches still warm from the bodies of enemy soldiers.

Yet another NVA company came charging through the forest, shattering trees with rockets and recoilless rifles. Our company was already rushing toward the grassy field, pulled in a rapid march toward the sound of enormous gunfire. Crashing through the brush at breakneck speed, we struggled to maintain group integrity, something vital in the kind of fight for which we were headed. The fight was already two hours in progress by the time we arrived on the eastern edge of the field. A Huey gunship swooped low and peppered the grass a few yards in front of us, bullets whizzed overhead from all directions, gunfire crackled all around, men shouted back and forth, the situation we walked into was total chaos. What's more, vision was very limited in the high grass.

Captain Harris ordered Lieutenant Proust to push us through the trenches until we got to the bivouac area, where we would link up with the Alpha Company platoon. Lane led the way into the trench, crouching so that all of his body was below the top of the waist-high ditch. Bent over that way, we were running fast in the trench when a tremendous explosion rattled us around like beads in a straw. It was an RPG. Suddenly, they were there right off our right flank.

A wave of fear swept over me. I threw a grenade as far as I could, then ducked below the trench. You have got to get your head up or you'll die, I thought, then rose up to shoot, and there was a Vietnamese man stumbling forward right in front of me. His clothes were all tattered and he was a bloody mess. I shot him just the same. Others behind him retreated to the grass and laid down a heavy volume of fire.

I looked around quickly to see who was dead or wounded, expecting that Lane had been killed by the RPG, but he was right there a few feet away, firing like everyone else in the squad.

"Machine gun up!" he shouted to Clark. Behind us I could hear Sergeant Wilson shout for us to "Get movin'," and for once I agreed with him. Why stay there where our position was known when we still had a lot of trench to use? With Clark and Hines pouring out covering fire from the M-60, we again moved along the trench in a high crawl.

The situation was all mixed up. NVA were inside our formations, attacking at some places and in retreat at others. We had a lot of different units coming from different directions at once, firefights erupting suddenly and ending abruptly, conflicting orders coming from the platoon commander and the company commander, and all the while shooting was going on all around. However, our platoon had one clear purpose in all the confusion: to break through to the besieged Alpha Company platoon.

With that in mind, we poured along the serpentine trench until it ran out at one of the mounds. There to greet us was an enemy machine gun, but the overanxious gunner fired too soon, when only a few men were out of the trench. Lemon fired two LAWs at the machine gun in quick succession and led his squad out of the trench in an assault on one side of the mound. I did not hear the enemy machine gun anymore, so I decided to take a chance. Lieutenant Proust called for us to stop, but no one paid him any attention. I ran at full speed, hit the ground, fired a few quick shots and rolled to the left, then got up and ran again. When I saw the rest of the squad behind me, I sprayed the mound to help cover their assault. Both squads came abreast and swept up the grass-covered mound in a line while the others followed in two columns that covered our flanks and rear.

I ducked quickly when we came over the top of the mound, then came to one knee and fired at the line of enemy troops below. Their backs to us, twenty or thirty NVA were firing at the Alpha Company platoon in the bivouac area under the trees. The heads and shoulders of two enemy soldiers in the grass about fifty yards directly below me showed well against the dark stand of trees farther away. I fired at them quickly, alternating my shots between the two, trying to kill them before they had a chance to turn and fire at me. "Get somebody from Alpha to cut off the right," Lane yelled, attempting to turn the tables on the enemy platoon and trap them between us and Alpha Company. I passed the message on to Abbot and fired at the same time. Enemy soldiers started to run to the right and left, offering only weak return fire as they went. Lieutenant Proust came to the top of the mound along with the other squads. Frost advised him that the enemy had presented us with a good opportunity by dividing themselves, that we could move down the small hill in two columns and encircle one group. The lieutenant ignored him and ordered us to stop shooting, fearing that we would hit someone in Alpha Company. He had orders to link up with the besieged platoon and ignored all else.

Behind us, two big tanks plowed over the mounds, drawing repeated strikes from B-40 rockets. "Gooks to the right," I heard Clark yell. Since all the friendlies were supposed to be to the left, I fired with impunity even though I could not see anyone in the tall grass. AKs cracked loudly as two rockets slashed out at the tanks. One rocket missed the tanks completely and the other glanced off the turret. The enemy troops who'd run to the left had circled around the mound to attack us from behind, as we had done to them. Wallace rushed his squad in front of the enemy to block their advance on the tanks. An enemy soldier burst from the grass and blasted Mitchell in the chest. The bullets came out of his back in a spout of red. From no more than fifteen feet, Gonzales answered with a blast of fire that ripped into the enemy soldier's chest and throat.

Realizing that they had no advantage, the enemy soldiers streamed down the small trench, heading right for the Delta Company position. In a well-rehearsed relay, I passed that information to Abbot and he quickly got the word to Delta Company. In the meantime, Lieutenant Proust got us moving down the hill toward the trees. As I rushed forward through the grass, an enemy soldier suddenly appeared at my feet. If he had not already been dead, he would have killed me. I kicked him in the head just the same and fired a couple of shots into his back.

At the bottom of the hill we dove for cover, forced to stop by gunfire that came at us from somewhere among the trees. Hurriedly, I called to Abbot and had him put the Alpha Company platoon on our frequency so we could tell which positions in the bivouac area were occupied by enemy troops. There were a lot of bunkers and trenches among the trees, some occupied by Marines but others, close by, held by NVA. However, I could make little sense of the radio operator's frantic descriptions, because he used landmarks we could not see. After a second or two of silence the radio operator came back with the message for us to "Hit the smoke!" In desperation, the radio operator had somehow gotten a smoke grenade on an enemy bunker. From alongside and behind the tanks we fired at the swirling purple smoke and moved forward as the Alpha platoon pulled back. Bullets pinged off the big metal monsters as we slowly forced our way into the camp. A blast from the cannon of the lead tank shattered the bunker, turning it into a shower of dirt and smoke. Frost rushed his squad into the breach and laid down a protective cover of fire to help the tanks move forward without the danger of some suicidal NVA soldier blowing them up.

The NVA opened up with a big .50 caliber machine gun, pocking the tanks with shallow holes, but doing little more than cosmetic damage. But one of the big bullets took off the lower part of Barnet's arm and burst open the side of his rib cage. Frost took off his shirt and wrapped it around the internal organs that were bulging from the big hole in the wounded man's side. The big machine gun sounded like a jackhammer, chopping away at us from some unseen place.

The tankers moved forward without infantry protection, and the 90mm shells not only destroyed the machine gun, but also drew enemy fire away from us and kicked up enough dust to conceal a quick rush forward by our platoon. In the wreckage of the bunker from which the machine gun fired, a wounded NVA soldier sat exposed from the waist up, his legs apparently trapped in the shattered timbers. With bullets flying all around him, he just sat there, not struggling to get free, nor did he bend over to make himself a smaller target. From behind trees and in holes, we fired at enemy troops in a line of bunkers. Meanwhile, the wounded NVA sat trapped in the bunker calmly awaiting death. I found myself hoping he would survive.

Four hours after the fight began, the last of our reserves joined in. Two platoons came all the way from Cam Lo, bringing two more tanks. The additional men and firepower turned the swirling battle in our favor. With tanks blasting away at the fortified positions, and the Delta Company platoons giving added support, we drove through the camp and linked up with the Alpha Company platoon. The NVA units in the bivouac area broke up and retreated in many different directions. Out on the grassy field, the other enemy units did the same. A mix of helicopter gunships and bird dogs harassed the enemy as they retreated.

By late evening the shooting had ended and all that was left was to count the dead. Ten Marines lost their lives in that hectic, confusing battle, and seventeen others were wounded. Surprisingly, both men from our platoon who were so severely wounded survived their injuries. The North Vietnamese Army left seventy-two dead men on the field and under the trees. Only one enemy soldier was taken alive, but he, too, died before the medevac helicopter reached Dong Ha.

I went to see if the wounded enemy soldier who was trapped in the bunker had survived, and when I got to the shattered little fortification, he was not there. I didn't ask anyone what happened to him, because it seemed inappropriate to show concern for the enemy when so many of our men had been killed and wounded and when passions were still running high.

Lemon had no such sense of embarrassment. "Did anybody see what happened to that dude who was settin' in the bunker?" he inquired loudly. "I sho was hopin' he would make it," he said without the slightest reservation. Much to my surprise, a lot of other guys in our platoon also empathized with the wounded enemy soldier; he was a symbol that we could live through even the worst predicaments. However, no one knew his fate. Possibly, in the chaos of the situation, some friend was able to rescue him, but it was more likely that he was among the stacks of enemy dead.

The Vietnamese had withdrawn in a very orderly manner, not in a panic or a rout. Despite the large number of bodies they left behind, they left none of their wounded and very few weapons. We found only four AK-47s, two old Chinese assault rifles, and the .50 caliber machine gun destroyed by the tank. Stores of ammunition were found in a few of the bunkers, but no significant caches.

With the enemy's intentions still unknown, the battalion headed for A4. When we were halfway home, the air began to resonate with the impact of exploding shells that searched for the scattered enemy troops. Even after Alpha Company marched off to Con Thien, A4 was still crowded with tired Marines. Sitting atop my bunker under an ever-darkening, overcast sky, I looked back over some of the ground we'd just covered to see what gashes the countryside had sustained, but everything looked quite the same; just like the war, it all stayed the same. Distant trees still swayed in the evening breeze, the grass still rippled like the waves on a windswept lake, and the destruction and death of a few hours earlier were nowhere seen. Temporarily, we had stopped the infiltration; temporarily, we had defeated the NVA; however, with the passage of very little time, it would all be the same.

Chapter 19

For the rest of the month, the vicinity of the grassy field was closely watched and periodically visited by small patrols from C2 and A4. However, as expected, no enemy activity was discovered. Even the big guns across the border were quiet during the latter part of April. Except for another visit by the division commander, it was business as usual. Lieutenant General Walt, Lieutenant General Cushman, and rifle-inspecting Major General Tompkins were greeted with resounding indifference by the troops. We knew that our fate did not rest in their hands; it was the generals across the river who decided where, when, and how we would fight. Most people just stayed out of sight as much as possible while the brass was in the base.

At 1645 on the same day as the generals' visit, two 120mm rockets roared into the base. The first dug a big hole in the LZ, and the second knocked over a mule (a small flatbed vehicle), wounding the driver. On the first of May a similar barrage of rockets did far more harm; one man was killed and another wounded. In the late morning of the following day, three more large rockets crashed into the base. The violent shudder of the bunker I was in said that the rockets had exploded somewhere in our sector of the perimeter. Abbot poked his head out of the bunker, then shouted back, "Somebody's hit," propelling us in a mad dash toward the twisted bodies sprawled in the dirt a few feet behind the bunker. Doc

White went to work trying to stop profuse bleeding from large cuts in Colbert's chest and arm. His legs were twisted like pretzels, broken in many places. He was barely conscious, hardly able to moan. Only the contorted grimace on his face communicated his deep agony. His crushed limbs immobilized, he was flown away, never to be seen again.

The following day I carried the radio for Frost's squad in an escort of trucks to and from Cam Lo. As we approached the south gate of A4 on the return trip, the west side of the perimeter erupted under a big artillery barrage, only the shells came from the south instead of the north. A two-hundred-mil deflection error by the 4/12 artillery battery had cost one man his life and left another paralyzed and dismembered. The wounded man lost part of one leg below the knee, and one arm was so mangled that it would be useless were it saved. The loss of life, the pain and suffering, were made even more tragic because it was inflicted by a mistake.

We thought we'd suffered another tragic mistake the following day when Hart and Brecht were fired on at OP2. Three sniper rounds from a nearby tree line sent them scurrying for cover. The 106mm recoilless rifle at the post sent a single shell whistling into trees less than one hundred yards away. Shell fragments and wood splinters burst into the air, some showering back onto the OP. Then two men darted back and forth among the trees and opened fire.

Two squads from our platoon were out at the OP site, creeping low among the trees and bushes in search of enemies in hiding. It did not take us long to come upon two bodies lying facedown among the cinders of burned brush. When I saw the USMC emblems on the sides of the flak jackets and helmets of the two dead men, I was horrified.

"My God! Two Marines have been killed by mistake!" Lane said, but before we could lament further, it was discovered that the two men in Marine Corps garb were Vietnamese. Though the ploy was one that had been used some months earlier in an attack on Con Thien, news of NVA troops dressed as Marines made everyone a bit more nervous. Passwords and codes were taken a lot more seriously after the discovery.

Two days later we had another encounter with enemy snipers. Two squads of our platoon patrolled each side of the road between A4 and C2. From very far to the east, ten shots kicked up dust along the road. We stopped and looked for the enemy, but found no one. We could tell that the shots were fired from a great distance because of the faint sound of the rifle. Using only sound as a guide, I called in a mission of 81mm mortars on the position from which I thought the shots might have come. A white phosphorous shell burst about five hundred yards away from the road, too far to be of any help to us, I thought; however, our own snipers saw someone move in the far-away brush. One of the Vietnamese snipers had moved when the noxious cloud of chemicals blew over his hiding place. Looking through powerful binoculars, the spotter in our sniper team discovered three NVA soldiers crouching low among the bushes. I took the binoculars with the intention of correcting the mortars to a more accurate position. Just as I focused on a single enemy soldier who squatted low in the bush, the crack of our sniper's big Winchester rang out. The enemy soldier's head snapped back violently in a spray of exploding tissue. Correcting from the last mortar round, I called in another mission near the dead enemy, again requesting WP. Another NVA made the mistake of trying to run away and was immediately shot down by our sniper. With two down and one to go, I called in another mission with HE. When no enemy was flushed, I switched to the 105mm cannons and called for VT (variable time) fuses. The airbursts spread shrapnel over a wide area, but still the third enemy soldier did not show himself. We started to resume our patrol, but Captain Harris ordered us to check out the results of our action. I made a feeble complaint about the possibility of other enemy soldiers being in the area, but he insisted that we do so. We really disliked doing that, because it added distance to the patrol.

Back at A4, the enemy across the border seemed to take our cue and exploded twelve airbursting shells over the base. Not since our stay in Gio Linh had I seen the enemy use airbursting shells. The day after that, something else happened that made us look to the sky for trouble. At 1015 in the morning of May 4, 1968, four big explosions rocked the center of the base and were followed by the clatter of machine-gun fire. Jolted by the sound of an unfamiliar weapon, I grabbed my rifle, dashed out of the bunker and into a trench.

"MiG! MiG!" shouted an anonymous voice from behind the bunker. Streaking toward the mountains to the northeast was a small delta-winged aircraft. "Corpsman up!" came the familiar shout that always followed tragedy. Along with both corpsmen in our platoon, I ran toward the call for help until we came to the countermeasures radar. This specialized radar system was highly effective at tracking incoming artillery and directing return fire. When we reached the radar, we found five badly wounded men sprawled around what was left of the apparatus. I was surprised no one had already reached the wounded men, because none of them was well enough to have called for help and other men were closer to the radar than us.

Desperately, I pressed a bandage against a large wound in the leg of one glassy-eyed man. The effort was insufficient; a large artery was pouring out his life, so I tied a tourniquet above the wound. That gave me an opportunity to attend the smaller wound in the man's chest. Against that wound I placed the foil side of the plastic package in which the bandage came and taped it as tightly as I could. With another man, Doc White pinched closed a wound in the man's side and pressed against it at the same time. Doc McDonald removed a large piece of metal from another man's throat. When the man still struggled to breathe, Doc McDonald cut a small hole in his throat, snapped a ballpoint pen in half, and jammed it into the hole. After Doc sucked out blood through the improvised trachea tube, the man began to breathe. For yet another wounded man there was no hope; his back was gashed with a multitude of large spurting wounds. Just the same, Doc McDonald worked feverishly, pumping at the man's chest to keep his heart working. Doc White slipped his shirt underneath the man's back to use as a big bandage, but it was too late; the young man died.

The death and destruction seemed to have been caused by two beam-riding antiradiation missiles that had homed in on the radar. Inside a circle of sandbags, the radar was left a wrecked mess of tangled wire and twisted metal. The big dish looked like a sieve. After the missiles struck, the small jet circled and fired a burst of machine-gun fire that also struck near the radar. Marines near the emplacement insisted that the small jet was a MiG-21 and they had fired at it when it made a second pass over the radar site. After some heated discussion, I tried to convince them that the small delta-winged jet was an A-4 Skyhawk, a ground attack aircraft. As I saw it, the Skyhawk was probably going after a missile site or radar-directed guns on the other side of the border and its missile picked up the signals from our radar and rode it into the base.

"Then why did he come around for a second pass?" someone asked.

"The pilot just followed his missiles to the target," I explained. I reminded him of all the other times that we'd been bombed or shelled by our own forces.

Lane insisted that this case was different, that there were too many landmarks to make such a mistake possible. The plane flew right over Con Thien coming in and going out. "A4 is right in the middle of a string of bases, you can see damn near to Dong Ha from the top of Con Thien," Lane contended, the implication being that the pilot had a good view of topography, which would have made it obvious he was on the wrong side of the border.

The more we argued, the more other people sided with Lane. "What kind of mission is that? Flak suppression by one plane?" Abbot asked skeptically. "I could go for your story, Gitch, but that second pass was too much to be a mistake, and that guy bugged out to the north. How many bases do we have to the north? Even if it came from a carrier, it would not go north," he said as most of the others started to gang up on me with questions like, What about the road? What about the air net (radio frequency)? What about the mountains?

Even though the error stretched normal reasoning, I still thought that the air strike on the radar was the result of the incompetence of a single pilot rather than an attack by the North Vietnamese. However, doubt started to creep into my mind. It did not seem reasonable that our radar would operate on the same frequency as the enemy's. All around were prominent terrain features, the Ben Hai River, the mountains to the northwest, the ocean to the east, the long line of fire support bases, any one of which should have put the pilot back on the correct course. How could such a thing happen in broad daylight? The NVA was certainly not lacking in boldness. After all, we'd just killed two enemy soldiers right on the edge of the base, they had a major infiltration route within sight of the base, and they were always full of surprises. Recalling the enemy troops in the American uniforms, I thought that the aircraft might have been a MiG-21 after all. The motive for the attack could have been due to the effectiveness of our counterartillery after the radar was installed; the radar tracked incoming artillery and directed our guns against enemy weapons. The big rocket attacks and the enemy sneaking close to the perimeter fit neatly with the supposition that the radar had become a big problem to the enemy. Most of the guys said that I did not want to believe that the plane was a MiG-21 because I was short and did not want something else to worry about.

We ended the debate about an hour after the air strike when six large rockets crashed into the center of the base. Throughout the afternoon the base shook under the explosions of incoming mortars and artillery. Almost from the moment the radar was destroyed, incoming artillery poured in on A4 and Con Thien. On May 5, 82mm mortars worked over A4 all day long. Shells started falling at 0300 and continued until 1315. The long barrage caused only one casualty, when a piece of shrapnel shattered the elbow of a guy from the first platoon as his squad returned from a night ambush.

After pounding our base all morning long, the gunners moved their attention to the next stop along the road. At 1400 five 120mm rockets and four big artillery shells crashed into C2 and wounded three men. The same pattern of bombardment was repeated the next day. At 0920 two men from our platoon were wounded by 82mm mortars as they returned to the base from a road sweep. At 1115 of the same day, another salvo of rockets sent us scurrying for cover. At 1130 nine more 82mm mortars fell upon us, and at 1154 two more. Again at 1230 four more 82mm shells fell at widely separated places around the base. Then at 1405 the big punch of eight 130mm artillery shells pounded the base, killing one man with two direct hits on one bunker. Again at 1640 three 82mm mortars exploded around the base. The final days of my tour of duty had come to look so much like the first. Like the days back at Gio Linh, life at A4 meant scurrying from one place to another in trenches, hoping that the capricious death from the sky would pass you by. The only thing that had changed in the last year was me. I had spent a month out of service, so my rotation date was in June instead of May.

As 2245 on May 6 an LP on the west side of the base saw ten enemy soldiers slip into a stand of trees a couple hundred yards away. NVA troops so close to the base had to signal the start of a ground attack, the three men thought as they rushed back to the perimeter. Our big 4.2 mortars plastered the small stand of trees, excavating all but a few. The base went on full alert, but no attack came. At dawn a search party found the bodies of two NVA among the splintered and broken trees. The audacious enemy soldiers were just passersby who used the base itself as concealment in the infiltration southward. The boldness of those men, passing within three hundred yards of the base, renewed debates about whether or not the CMR was destroyed by a MiG-21 or an A-4 Skyhawk.

On May 7 we were awakened by three rounds of 100mm artillery and three 82mm mortar rounds. Minutes later two VT rounds exploded overhead and sent a shower of propaganda leaflets fluttering to the ground. Souvenir hunters rushed to grab the leaflets, but an unfortunate wind blew most of the papers beyond the wire. At 1605 of the same day, three rounds of 82mm struck at A4, then twelve more hit at 1800. The constant bombardment decreased the scope of our offensive operations, limiting the effectiveness of our artillery and making travel near the base hazardous. Most of all it sowed tension in the daily lives of the troops. Later in the night of May 7, at 2235, another LP on the west side of the base spotted five figures moving among the bushes. With no adjustment, 4.2 mortars fell on the bushes that concealed the enemy. Gunfire from the LP sent everyone scrambling to fighting stations with expectations of exchanging fire with the enemy, but nothing happened. A search in the darkness did not find any enemy soldiers. Though one of the NVA soldiers dropped a rifle in his flight through the darkness, they had successfully slipped past us.

Another small group of NVA was not as successful. As they moved through the grassy field, they ran head-on into a squad from Alpha Company that was on its way to an ambush site. In the early-morning darkness, a furious close-quarter shoot-out left two NVA soldiers dead and one Marine wounded. The Marines took the weapons from the dead, an AK-47 and an AK-51, and headed straight for A4. As they approached the base they were hurried along by an incoming salvo of 82mm mortars.

At noon on May 8 the base was again shaken by a long barrage of incoming artillery. By this time, considering the dangers of contact with enemy troops to be less than those of the incessant shelling, I took every opportunity that I could to get out of the base. Just as I returned from a supply run to Cam Lo, incoming 82mm mortars sent us diving for cover among the ditches just outside the gate to A4. No one was hurt, but the truck on which I'd arrived was completely destroyed. To die after going through so much seemed so profane and unfair.

The next day, OP1 sighted four NVA following a path similar to the one used by another group who slipped past the base the previous day. As penalty for the repetition, they were trapped by brackets of 60mm mortars and bullets from the OP. Other enemy troops were nearby, and they responded with 60mm mortars of their own. But the NVA's mortars did little to help the trapped NVA troops. Our platoon swept through the area as soon as the barrage of small mortars was lifted, searching the bush ahead of us with gunfire. When morning came, we found the bodies of three enemy troops. We expected to go hunting for the others who fired the mortars into the base, but were assigned to patrol the road as usual.

An Alpha Company squad that patrolled the road between Con Thien and A4 spotted three NVA troops moving away from them to the west. Too far away for the squad to effectively use their rifles, they radioed another squad, which carried snipers along with them. From almost a thousand yards away our sniper fired a shot that burst into the back of one of the enemy soldiers. The others disappeared into the bush before bullets could search them out.

After the counterbattery radar was destroyed, the enemy moved some heavy weapons close to the base, more accurately continuing the rain of 82mm mortars that constantly pounded us. On May 9 the enemy got close enough to use recoilless rifles. The flat trajectory of that weapon was particularly effective against bunkers. Our counterfire at suspected enemy positions seemed to have very little effect on the continuous stream of incoming shells. At dawn on May 10 the base trembled under a forty-round barrage of big rockets and heavy artillery. Two air-exploding VT rounds slightly wounded three men who were crouched in a trench, just business as usual at A4. Later in the morning, OP1 saw two NVA troops and fired at them. As usual, the enemy soldiers did not return the fire, only ran away quickly. Why the enemy would come so close to the base with no intention of shooting at us perplexed us.

Later in the evening, one of our snipers went out to OP1. Searching with a starlight scope, he saw a single NVA soldier standing at the edge of a clearing casually surveying the area ahead of him. With his rifle slung over his shoulder and his hands on his hips, the enemy scout clearly sensed no danger. He stood calmly until an M-14 bullet exploded into his chest. A flurry of return gunfire from behind the dead scout had our sniper cringing behind sandbags while the two riflemen discouraged the enemy with steady return fire. A squad from the base rushed out to the OP and threw all of their firepower at the enemy, quickly chasing them away. On the way back to the base, the squad experienced one of the oddities of fate that seemed so much more common in Vietnam. Our sniper who had just moments earlier claimed a victim was himself victimized by an enemy sniper, struck in the back by a single shot. Two well-placed 82mm mortars interfered with the medevac helicopter that came quickly to take away the wounded sniper.

At sunrise most of the company was out in the area of the brief firefight, to sweep the bush in search of the enemy. Enemy soldiers at the very edge of the base was apparently too much for our commanders to tolerate, yet so many soldiers on such a petty mission seemed inappropriate. The overcommitment became clear when later in the afternoon we were graced by another visit by Generals Tompkins and Davis. Our generals had nothing to fear from snipers, for true to course, their visit was almost entirely underground in the company CP bunker. Just the same, in light of all the artillery that pounded the base every day, their visit was quite remarkable. We hoped that they had come with some new plan to counter the incessant hammering we took from enemy artillery. But no such operation came.

Chapter 20

On May 14 I took escort duty on a small convoy of trucks headed up to Con Thien so I could visit some of my old friends in Alpha Company before they left for Khe Sanh. Alfred, also a short-timer, was as jovial and witty as the first time we met out on the nearby firebreak many months before. Incoming 82mm mortar shells cut short our reminiscences about others who had gone before us, like Chambers and Big Fifty. The truckers were particularly anxious to get out of range of the big guns along the border, so the supplies were unloaded quickly.

While we worked on that detail, a circling bird dog spotted two NVA soldiers in the bush west of the base. Two squads were sent to search, and the rest of the company was placed on full alert; that ended my visit. In their search of the bush, the Marines stumbled upon another group of enemy soldiers and immediately took them under fire. The Marines quickly came on line and laid down an intense volley of fire that pinned down the enemy troops. The Marines then walked in 81mm mortars from behind the enemy position and prepared to assault any weakness that showed itself, but the enemy called in 82mm mortars, which wounded one Marine and forced the others back. When the mortar barrage lifted, the Marines rushed forward again, only to be stopped by the explosion of three big 130mm shells. The Marines made their way to A4 with explosions chasing them all the way.

Just after dark on May 17 Frost's squad left the base headed for an ambush site on the edge of the grassy field near the place of our last large-scale fight. I carried the radio. About an hour after we left, we heard movement in the tall grass. It was not necessary to pass word of impending danger, because all of us heard the noise. In the dark, moonless night, we could see no one and could not tell the exact direction from which the noise came. Just the same, we sprang the ambush when the sound grew louder. The unseen enemy fired back desperately. We shot at each other for about five minutes, neither side knowing exactly where the other was. The shooting stopped abruptly, and all I could hear was a strong wind in the grass. Then there was moaning, long and loud.

Since we were unsure about the size of the unit we had ambushed, we crept slowly away to a safer position about a hundred yards away and waited for morning. At first light we went back to the place where the shooting happened and found three dead enemy soldiers on the blood-soaked grass. Creeping low and quietly, we followed a trail of blood in search of wounded enemy soldiers who might have escaped the ambush. Douglas led the single-file column, pointing a .45 before him. Suddenly, he jumped to one side and fired three quick shots. A few feet ahead of him lay a dead enemy soldier. Though all of Douglas's shots had found the mark, they were superfluous, because the enemy soldier was already cold, dead from the ambush late in the night. We took his weapon and papers and started back for A4, but were diverted by yet another bloody trail. Cautiously, we followed it through the grass until Insuranceman quietly whispered the discovery of a spider trap. Frost crawled to the back of the grass-covered pit and pulled open the hatch. From one side, Douglas and Insuranceman poured bullets into the hole. Inside the hole, a North Vietnamese soldier was shot about fifty times but, incredibly, was still alive. Douglas started to pull him out of the hole, but Frost said not to bother, then told Insuranceman to "finish him." Insuranceman took the pistol from Douglas and dispatched the enemy with a single shot to the front of his head. It was a mercy killing to spare him any further suffering. After taking the dead man's weapon, a 7.62 PPS submachine gun, Douglas closed the lid to the spider trap, making it the dead man's grave.

Back at A4 we celebrated the success of our ambush with a lot of revelry. The occasion quickly turned into a farewell party for me, a kind of ritualized "This Is Your Life" that often was the send-off for those headed home. My rotation date had finally come. All I had to do was catch the supply truck back to Dong Ha the next morning.

Late afternoon of that same day, a platoon from Delta Company stumbled into an NVA platoon southeast of C2. In the fierce firefight that ensued, both sides shifted rapidly to try to gain advantage over the other. In encounters between units of similar size, Americans usually had an advantage because of superior firepower; however, in Quang Tri Province the enemy could call upon nearly all the supporting heavy weapons that we could. When the Delta Company platoon called in artillery, the NVA platoon returned the favor. A bird dog was quickly in action to help direct artillery onto the enemy. Instead of bringing good news, the AO reported that another NVA platoon was on the way to help their comrades. The Marines were given a frantic call to pull back before they were trapped. However, the warning did not come soon enough and the Marines were quickly surrounded. When word came to "saddle up," I put on my radio and grabbed extra ammunition in anticipation of a long fight. Everyone thought I was crazy for going along with the platoon, because I did not have to go.

"Stay behind," Abbot implored. "I don't want you to

die," he said, almost with tears in his eyes. What he did not understand, nor did I, was at that point I did not much care if I died. Lane expected that I would join the squad instead of staying behind. In a column formation, we trotted along toward the sound of the distant guns. The movements were automatic for me. I was not going back to the World, this *was* the World.

When the fight first began, the Delta Company platoon divided into two wedge formations and attacked from two different directions. To avoid being cut in two, the NVA platoon rapidly retreated and fired at one of the Marine formations until their friends arrived. When the other NVA platoon arrived at the scene, it looped around the first Marine formation. The other Marine formation attacked as the enemy knew they would, so the NVA just moved out of the way and let them join the trapped group and encircled both. The Marines easily broke out of the trap by focusing their fire on one point in the thin circle of enemy troops.

For all the shooting and maneuvering, I had not heard a word of casualties, so I assumed that the situation toward which we rushed was not very desperate. A curtain of artillery blocked the retreat of the enemy to the east unless they broke up into small groups. If they did that with so many American troops in the area, the small groups would be very vulnerable. In a plan formulated on the run, our company was to attack the NVA from the north and drive them into a Delta Company blocking force to the south. We moved quickly through the thin brush, each platoon parallel to the other in a fast march spread over a wide area.

Out on point, Lemon and Colletta brought our columns to a quick halt with long bursts of fire from their M-16s. Smoke from enemy rifles rose just a few yards ahead of the column. The surrounding terrain offered little cover except for a few scattered mounds of earth. Our quick arrival had surprised one of the enemy platoons, which tried to escape to the north. Over the radio, Captain Harris shouted orders for the other platoons to close in on our position, giving them precise routes so that we would not shoot each other. Lieutenant Proust radioed for Lane to move his squad to the left. He was right. We had to spread out more for our fire to be more effective, but the bullets whistling through the bush discouraged any movement. I crawled over the gravel for about twenty yards like a lizard over a hot rock, then fired at a man I saw get up and run. He went down, either from my bullets or because it was the sensible thing to do.

The second platoon arrived in a hail of gunfire. Over the radio, the Delta Company platoon shouted that we were firing into their position. The captain ordered us to cease fire while the Delta troops moved. Quick to exploit every opportunity, the Vietnamese rushed to a more advantageous position about a hundred yards to their rear as our fire slackened.

Though they had better cover among the small gullies, they had a lot less concealment. Without any orders to do so, our platoon moved forward until there was more than fifty yards between us and the enemy. A well-placed M-79 round fell into a depression from which three enemy soldiers were firing. One of them, his arm nearly severed, stumbled out of the shallow hole and was shot several more times. Still he kept fighting, until a string of bullets walked up his back. The second platoon kept pouring grenades from one side while we kept up heavy firing. Instinctively, I could feel the NVA return fire grow weaker by the minute. A few feet from me, a bullet struck Dupont on the top of his head and came out under his chin. Amazingly, he did not die, and even stayed conscious.

Lemon fired a LAW into a small mound of earth from behind which a group of enemy soldiers had taken cover, sending up a geyser of shrapnel and debris that threatened us as well as the enemy. We had them and were tearing them to pieces. Then suddenly the dull *thump* of a big machine gun constricted me with terror. Bullets from the machine gun lashed through the folds of earth like it was not there. A single bullet struck Parez in the foot and took it right off. Another exploded into Catman's chest, killing him almost instantly. Lemon threw caution to the wind, stood up and fired two LAWs in the direction of the machine gun. Under the cover of smoke and dust that followed, we beat a hasty retreat for about a hundred yards to the rear. We did not move farther, for fear that we would lose contact.

We tried to pin them down and let the second platoon close in from one side, but the machine gun kept us scrambling for cover and allowed part of the enemy force to withdraw. The crackle of enemy rifles grew dimmer until little else but the big machine gun could be heard from the NVA side of the fight. We automatically moved forward again. When the machine gun paid particular attention to one place, Marines at another would scurry forward a few feet. It became clear that the machine gun could not hold back so many troops spread out over a wide area. That recognized, I was startled by Lieutenant Proust's order for us to hold fast.

Every passing minute meant that the enemy got farther away. After what seemed like a century, a tank crashed through the bush behind us. With bullets splashing harmlessly over its thick armor, the tank's 90mm cannon roared several times in search of the enemy machine gun. Using the tank for cover, Lane's squad moved slowly forward until we were at the gully from which the enemy had fired. The turret of the tank swept back and forth, raking the area with coaxial machine-gun fire. The other squads rushed through the bush while we surrounded the tank to protect it from the possibility of a suicidal sapper who might try to take it out. The whole platoon had been held up by just three enemy troops and a .50 caliber machine gun, all of which were destroyed by the tank.

With the way cleared of that obstruction, we again went in hot pursuit of the enemy. The North Vietnamese tendency to stand and fight was working against them. Just past the row of small washes and gullies, the enemy platoon, or what remained of it, had taken up position in a long trench that circled around the edge of a wide clearing. The tank commander did not want to cross the gullies, so our squad had to escort it around the barrier. In the meantime the rest of the platoon pushed through bushes and small trees and again made contact with the enemy platoon. Throwing everything they had, LAWs, grenades, M-79s, Wallace's squad fought its way into one portion of the trench in a quick frontal assault. Lieutenant Proust ordered them to pull back and wait for the tank, but a bullet that struck the platoon commander in the butt canceled that order. The platoon kept up the pressure on the ever-weakening enemy. By the time we arrived with the tank, the enemy was in complete disarray, trying desperately to scatter as they dashed from the trench. The tank roared across the clearing, but it could not fire because Marines were between it and the enemy. While other squads pushed forward, cutting down small groups of enemy soldiers who tried to slow their advance, Lane's squad rushed into the trench to cover the rear.

Running at full speed to catch up to the tank, we plunged into the trench and spread out quickly. Insuranceman and I ducked into a bunker at one end of the trench to put our rifles through its gun ports, but from just inside the hatchway gunfire sent us leaping to the floor. In a panic, I switched my rifle to fully automatic with the flick of a thumb and filled the bunker with bullets. Bullets ricocheted all around the small enclosure and the room filled with smoke. Over my shoulder, Insuranceman fired the same way I did, and still the enemy in the darkness was somehow able to shoot back. With the nimblest fingers and a flick of the wrist, I slipped in another clip and again

pumped bullets all around. Had it not been for the fact that
the earthen walls absorbed so much of the lead, I might
have been killed by my own shots. In the smoke and darkness I could see nothing, not even muzzle flashes, but soon
realized that only Insuranceman and I were shooting. I
backed out of the bunker without even touching my team-
mate, then jumped out of the trench. Lane and three others
circled the bunker with their rifles at the ready in case the
wrong person came out. A few seconds later Insuranceman
came out, dragging a dead NVA soldier with him. In spite
of all the shooting at such close range, the dead man had
been hit only four or five times; fortunately, two of the hits
were to the head. Three men in an eight-by-ten room
shooting at each other with automatic weapons, it was
amazing that we all weren't killed!

In the meantime the other squads had nearly wiped out
what was left of the enemy platoon, and came back to the
trench to await the arrival of the other platoons so we
could continue the advance in concert with the rest of the
company. As they returned, I watched an F-4 Phantom
roll in from the east and streak toward us trailing a stream
of black smoke, presumably to finish off some part of the
enemy platoon that had found refuge nearby. I was jolted
with terror when two silver cocoons dropped from underneath the wings of the screaming jet and tumbled straight
toward us. Screaming "Incoming!" I dove into the trench
and scrambled toward the bunker. The men in our squad
instinctively lunged for the trench upon hearing my
warning. In a flash of horror, a fiery inferno covered the
field with a hellish nightmare. It looked as if we'd been
thrown into the middle of the sun. The heat was excruci-
ating and the gas suffocating. Completely engulfed in
flames, a Marine who had not made it to the trench
screamed loudly as he stumbled about. Doc White
knocked him over and rolled him around in the grass to
put out the flames. The trench did not mean safety for
everyone. One man in the trench was charred black by a

splash of napalm, burned so badly that he was hardly recognizable. His eyes were burned out and his face was just
flaking tatters of skin. Nothing smells worse than the
burned flesh of a living person. We'd taken the enemy
position so quickly that no one had called off the air
strike.

As if that tragedy were not bad enough, enemy fire
again came at us across a broad front. The pop and clatter
of enemy rifles signaled the approach of an even larger
enemy force than we'd just defeated. Sergeant Wilson
frantically called for the tank to return and for the second
platoon to come along with it. The whole company
rushed to our aid and engaged the enemy across a broad
front. Instead of closing to the short range from which
they usually fought, the large enemy force fired at us
from a great distance. The remainder of Delta Company
came from C2 and Cam Lo. Two platoons from 2/26
were brought in by helicopter. After it dropped off a load
of troops, a HU-46 was shot down when it started to lift
off. The rear of the two big rotors was torn into fragments, causing the big troop-carrying helicopter to crash
to earth on its side. Our company stayed put, acting as a
blocking force as other Marines closed in on the enemy
from two different directions. The NVA broke contact,
using a big barrage of artillery fire to discourage the
Marines from following.

For our platoon, the long day of brutal fighting ended
with the stench of napalm and burned flesh still swirling in
the air. Mercifully, the two men who were so badly burned
died before a medevac helicopter could take them away. In
all, four men from our platoon had been killed and six
wounded. When all of our casualties were counted, forty
Marines were dead and thirty were wounded, but the
battle had been a disaster for the North Vietnamese, who
left three hundred dead and a wealth of weapons on the
battlefield.

Back at the base, we talked little of the victory,

possibly because we were so drained by the fight. There was all the usual stuff to be done, watch rotations, radio watch, LPs, and the rest. The next day, instead of riding back to Dong Ha on the supply truck, I rode in a helicopter along with the bodies of two men who had been killed in an artillery barrage the previous day. Below, the DMZ was a moonscape of craters, scarred by years of war.

For me, the fighting was over. In three days I would be in Okinawa, and another week still, I would walk the streets of San Francisco. When the helicopter landed at Dong Ha, I helped them unload the dead men, ending my tour of duty the way it had started.

Appendix

Marine Artillery Capabilities

WEAPONS	RANGE (meters)	WEIGHT (pounds)	SUSTAINED RATE OF FIRE PER MINUTE	PRIME MOVER	EFFECTIVE AREA OF BURST (meters, one round) DEPTH	WIDTH	AMMUNITION TYPES AVAILABLE	FUZES AVAILABLE	WEIGHT OF FUZED HE PROJO (pounds)	FINAL PROTECTIVE FIRE
105mm How Towed M101A1	11,000	4,980	3	Helo 2½-ton truck	20	30		Q,D TI VT CP	33	200
155mm How Towed M114A1	14,600	12,950	1	Helo 5-ton truck	30	50	HE L HE Illum WP Smoke RAP Gas Nuclear	Q,D TI VT CP	95	300
155mm How (SP) M109A1	14,600	53,060	1	SP	30	50				
8" How (SP) M110	16,800	58,500	0.5	SP	30	80	HE Spot Gas Nuclear	Q,D TI VT CP	200	N/A
155mm Gun (SP) M53	23,500	96,000	0.5	SP	30	50		Q,D VT	95	N/A
107mm Mort M30	5,656	671	15–20	Helo ¾-ton truck	30	30	Illum WP Gas	Q,D TI VT	26	200

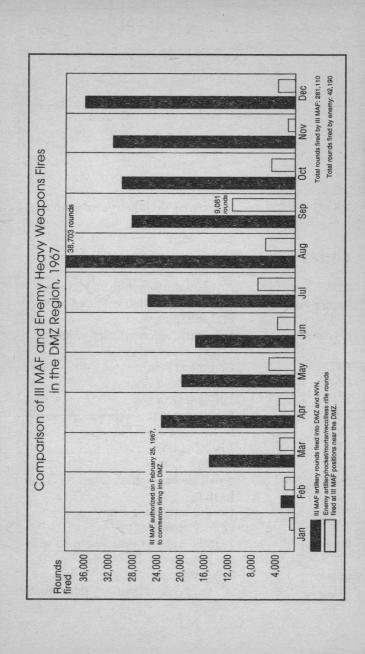

Comparison of III MAF and Enemy Heavy Weapons Fires
in the DMZ Region, 1967

Rounds fired

III MAF artillery rounds fired into DMZ and NVN.

Enemy artillery/rocket/mortar/recoilless rifle rounds
fired at III MAF positions near the DMZ.

III MAF authorized on February 25, 1967,
to commence firing into DMZ.

38,703 rounds

9,081 rounds

Total rounds fired by III MAF: 281,110

Total rounds fired by enemy: 42,190

Glossary

AK-47	Automatic assault rifle in common use by both the VC and NVA by the early 1960s
Arc-Light	Operational name for B-52 strikes in South Vietnam
ARVN	Army of the Republic of Vietnam
bangalore torpedo	Bamboo pole filled with explosives
C-4	Plastic explosive
claymore	U.S.-built electronically detonated antipersonnel mine
CP	Command Post
DMZ	Demilitarized Zone
FO	Forward Observer
LAW	Light Antitank Weapon. A small rocket encased in Fiberglas
LP	Listening Post
LZ	Landing Zone
mule	Small flatbed vehicle used for light hauling
NVA	North Vietnamese Army
OP	Observation Post
Ontos	Lightly armored vehicle armed with six 106mm recoilless rifles
pogue	A person in a soft job
PRC-25	A twenty-five-pound field pack radio

RPG Rocket Propelled Grenade launcher. A small antitank weapon that VC and NVA used effectively against fortified positions

sit-rep Situation report

TPQ Ground-based radar system used to guide aircraft on bombing missions

VT Variable Timed fuse. Usually used to make artillery shells explode in the air